ALTERNATIVE HEALTH

MASSAGE

The Author

Jolanta Basnyet is the Principal of the Lancashire Holistic College and proprietor of the Natural Health Centre in Preston, England. She holds professional qualifications in the fields of Body Massage, Aromatherapy and Reflexology and is vice-chairman of the British Massage Therapy Council. She is also a qualified osteopath and registered with the Guild of Osteopaths and The Institute for Complementary Medicine. Jolanta has gained considerable experience over many years as a lecturer and practitioner. She is the author of *Healing by Feeling* and has produced video cassettes on Body Massage, Aromatherapy and Reflexology. She enjoys teaching and training future practitioners.

The Institute for Complementary Medicine

The Institute for Complementary Medicine (ICM) was founded in Britain in 1982. It is a charitable organization whose aim is to encourage the development of all forms of complementary medicine, including research, education and standards of clinical practise, and to provide factual information to the media and the public. With over 370 affiliated organizations, the ICM sees complementary medicine as a separate and independent source of health care, yet it always encourages a correct relationship with the medical profession to ensure each case receives the most appropriate treatment available.

ALTERNATIVE HEALTH

MASSAGE

JOLANTA BASNYET

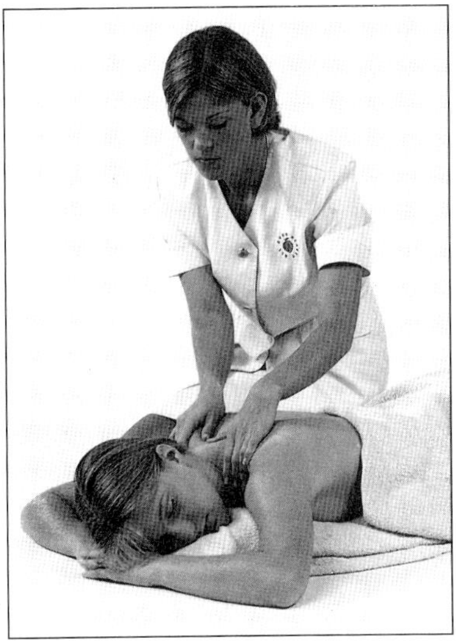

GREENWICH EDITIONS

A Salamander Book

This edition published by Greenwich Editions
10 Blenheim Court, Brewery Road
London N7 9NT
United Kingdom.

ISBN 0 86288 265 6

9 8 7 6 5 4 3 2 1

All correspondence concerning this volume should be addressed to Salamander Books Ltd.

This book was created by SP Creative Design for Salamander Books Ltd.
Editor: Heather Thomas
Designer: Al Rockall
Production: Rolando Ugolini
Illustration reproduction: Emirates Printing Press, Dubai
Printed in Spain

Photography:
Studio photography by Bruce Head
The Image Bank: page 24

Acknowledgments:
The publishers would like to thank the following for their kind assistance in producing this book:
Staff from All Over Beauty, Bury St Edmunds
Lotte Amery, Pam Chappell and Thomas, Ian Croft, Lynsey Fidler, Rebecca Hartley

IMPORTANT
The information, recipes and remedies contained in this book are generally applicable and appropriate in most cases, but are not tailored to specific circumstances or individuals. The authors and publishers cannot be held responsible for any problems arising from the mistaken identity of any plants or remedies, or the inappropriate use of any remedy or recipe. Do not undertake any form of self diagnosis or treatment for serious complaints without first seeking professional advice. Always seek professional medical advice if symptoms persist.When dealing with pregnancy or infants, special care should be exercised and the advice of the midwife or GP obtained.

CONTENTS

MASSAGE THERAPY

Body massage can be described as the manipulation of soft tissue for therapeutic purposes. However, musculo-skeletal disorders can also be treated with soft tissue manipulation, i.e. body massage. In general terms, these technicalities are of minor importance and in this book we shall concentrate mainly on the different types of body massage which are used to create a specific effect.

During a family holiday in Nepal, I came across an unusual sight. After a few days touring the Kathmandu valley, we decided to travel to the Gaida Park in the Terrai Region where there are splendid examples of the tropical flora and fauna indigenous only to the Himalayas. On the way, we stopped for lunch in a small restaurant perched on top of a hill above a breathtaking ravine. All around us were Japanese tourists, old and young, male and female, and the people sitting down were being massaged by others standing behind them, rubbing their shoulders and neck areas. The old were massaging the young, and the teenagers were massaging the heads, scalps and backs of the more elderly tourists while they waited for their meal.

The Japanese were even working on each other's feet while sitting on the floor in the ladies' room. Taking turns, they were giving each other gentle, relaxing massage treatment not only on the shoulders and neck but also on the feet to relax them even more. They did not waste their time waiting idly at the table; they were trying to relieve and banish travel fatigue and tiredness. After their meal, they left for their coach, relaxed and refreshed.

COMBATING STRESS

Stress is the body's worst enemy and we all need to learn effective methods of stress management. Stress is the main cause of illness in the body, and body massage can successfully treat modern illnesses, such as tension, aches and pains, insomnia and headaches, all of which are accumulated in the course of daily life.

EVERYONE CAN BENEFIT

Body massage is a part of Ayurvedic medicine. A good example is the emotional closeness between a mother and her baby. Massage can make the bond between them even stronger because of the well-established and natural tactile contact. Massaging and rubbing are almost an instinctive part of their relationship. In

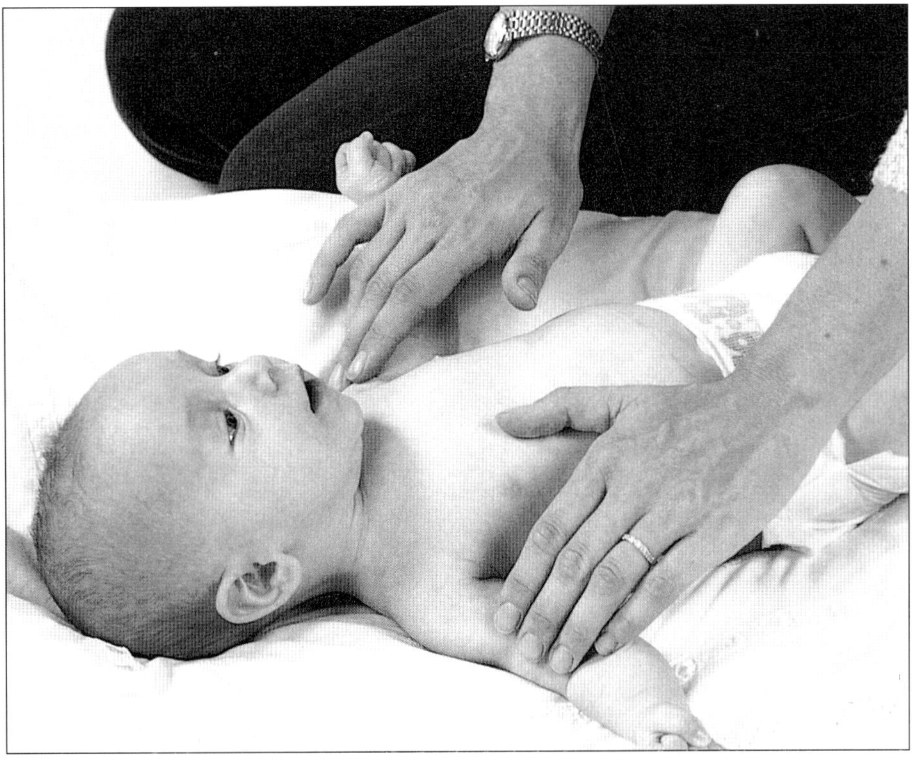

Nepal and India, babies are massaged daily as part of their nursing routine, either by their mothers or by nannies. However, in Western society, we have only recently started to appreciate the benefits of massage treatment which can help to de-stress the body and relax it sufficiently to cope with everyday problems and even the stress of major decision-making processes.

We develop our sense of touch from our inception. Human embryos are photographed sucking their thumbs in their mothers' wombs. From birth to old age, we receive tactile stimuli on a regular basis. All infants develop a powerful sense of touch, both emotionally and physically. In fact, touch is usually their first contact with their mother, providing a unique closeness which grows even stronger with the passing of time. At the other end of the spectrum, in old age, any physical contact is much appreciated, and numerous research studies confirm that when tactile contact is frequent, elderly patients have less need of painkillers and sleeping tablets.

Above: everybody can benefit from massage, even babies.

A TWO-WAY PROCESS

People denied frequent physical contact can feel lonely, rejected, depressed and isolated. Body massage consists of touch, and touch means contact. However, massage is a two-way process of tactile experience – hence the hands of the giver and the skin of the receiver are very much aware of each other. They have to work together and this tactile understanding and co-operation can be a very emotional and powerful experience.

EARLY MEDICINE

It was the ancient Greek physician Hippocrates, the so-called 'father of modern medicine', who first recognised the beneficial action of body massage. He said that 'rubbing can bind a joint that is too loose, and loosen a joint that is too rigid. Hard rubbing binds, much rubbing causes parts to waste, and moderate rubbing makes them grow.'

This was pronounced as the ultimate truth in the fifth century BC. Most of the doctors in ancient times had some knowledge of herbs, oils, massage and other forms of natural treatment. In fact, medicine, as it was then, was preventative rather than purely curative as it is now in our Western culture.

Doctors tried to prevent illness and keep their patients in a good state of health; otherwise they were not paid their fees. If they suffered a loss of earnings, there was a decline in the number of patients. Hence, they travelled around the country to escape their reputation for failures and to tout for new business. However, their infamy sometimes accompanied them, and some of the most unfortunate ones even went abroad.

It was a natural process of elimination. The inferior professional advice and treatment offered by poorly qualified doctors was gradually eradicated through a process of 'natural cleansing'. In order to maintain high standards in medical training, qualifications and knowledge, the 'poor-quality' doctors were prevented from practising.

ELIMINATING WASTE!

The Roman physician Galen, who lived in the second century AD, wrote many books relating to massage and exercise and advocated massage for the gladiators. He stated that massage 'eliminates the waste products of nutrition and the poisons of fatigue'.

THE ORIGINS OF MASSAGE

The word massage, according to one school of thought, originated from the Greek word *massein*, meaning 'to knead'. However, it may be derived from the Arabic word *mass*, or *mas'h*, meaning 'to press softly'.

What we do know is that body massage is one of the oldest forms of natural treatment for many human ailments and disorders, since it is an instinctive human reaction to hold or rub painful parts of the body. How often do you see a crying child who has fallen over being consoled by an

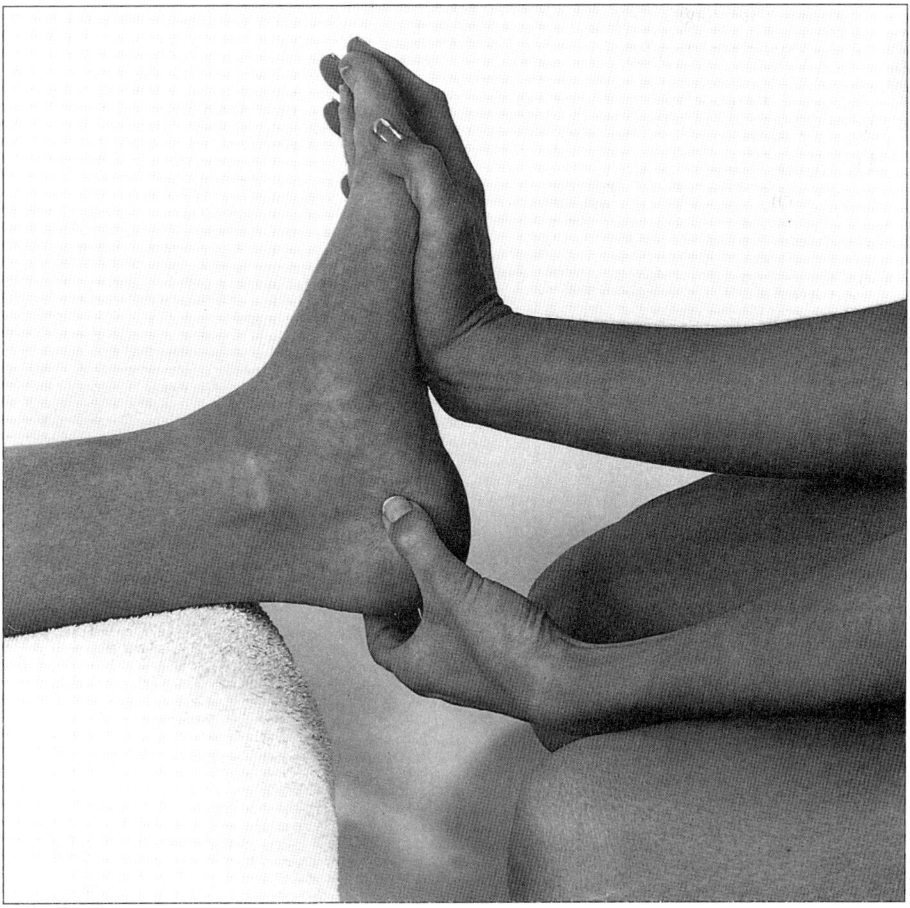

adult rubbing the aching part or even kissing it 'to make it better'? The origin of this word is not as important as the knowledge that, as an art of healing, massage is as old as man himself.

The Chinese had a system of body massage 5,000 years ago as did the Hindus, the Japanese and the ancient Egyptians. Chinese priests maintained that 'early morning effleurage after a night's sleep protects against cold, keeps the organs supple and prevents minor ailments'.

Above: the whole body can gain from the therapeutic and relaxing effects of massage, including the feet.

The Hindus, however, believed that 'massage reduces fat, strengthens the muscle and firms the skin'. Even today we cannot argue with this statement. Multiple research studies indicate that massage treatment is beneficial for increasing muscle tone and breaking up adipose tissues in the body. Consequently, massage treatment is ideal for healthy people who wish to maintain their good health as well as those who want to increase their level of fitness. As the Arab proverb states: 'He who has health has hope; and he who has hope has everything'. This maxim should be remembered when we discuss the beneficial effects of body massage treatment.

THE BIRTH OF MODERN MASSAGE

It was unfortunate that the teachings of the Catholic Church and the religious crusades of the Middle Ages precluded the use of massage and stopped the further development of tactile natural therapies. However, in the early nineteenth century, a Swedish professor called Peter Ling (1776–1839) developed a more scientific approach to massage and exercise. This type of therapeutic treatment was based on the physiological functions of the human body. In 1820, Ling established an institute in Stockholm where massage was taught. He was the originator of the modern concept of massage, known as Swedish Body Massage, but it was a long time before massage became generally accepted by the medical profession as a form of therapeutic treatment.

THERAPEUTIC MASSAGE

Massage therapy is growing in popularity and its benefits are well known. Many colleges and training establishments offer massage courses where you can be taught the way to touch and the way to heal through touch. Healing touch does not have to be performed by an experienced therapist. Touch is healing. However, in order to achieve a particular therapeutic aim, the healing touch has to be made more specific. It has to employ therapeutic techniques which can enhance the treatment in remedial terms.

There are many types of massage which are recognised and taught as specific forms of discipline, including classical Swedish Body Massage, Shiatsu Massage, Baby Massage, Remedial Massage, Neuromuscular Massage, Biodynamic Massage and Massage for Sports Injuries. We also recognise Manual Lymph Drainage within massage therapy as well as aromatherapy and sensual massage. Some 'hands-on' bodywork therapies, such as Rolfing and the Rosen Method, may display a different approach but they still relate to the human body in its physical appearance, physiological functions and mental processes.

COMPLEMENTARY MEDICINE

The most up-to-date statistical figures indicate that one in ten people in Britain consults a practitioner of natural therapies each year. In France, more than a third of the population use some form of complementary medicine. In Japan, two-thirds of the population claim they use non-conventional treatments. Interest in complementary medicine is growing on a world-wide basis.

AIMS AND BENEFITS OF MASSAGE

There have been numerous research studies in the field of massage and their findings are impressive. Some of them are of a clinical nature but most research projects are not conducted in a controlled scientific environment.

■ There is substantial evidence that massage has pain-relieving effects associated with skin stimulation and increased temperature. Decreased muscle tension and stimulation of the peripheral nerve endings also bring pain relief.

■ All these effects help induce relaxation, both mentally and physically. For example, a study that was conducted in a hospice environment suggested that massage reduced anxiety scores.

■ Research suggests that infants receiving touch stimulation may perform better in relation to weight gain, height, decreased incidence of respiratory problems and better digestion.

■ Findings in the field of sports injuries suggest that healing is faster in people who receive massage.

■ Massage can help reduce anxiety, and psychological relaxation can occur even in the absence of physiological relaxation.

■ Digestion may be stimulated and digestive processes are better balanced when using massage – in this instance, infants react to massage extremely favourably.

■ Blood flow is increased during the process of massage, and the stimulated amount of blood carries oxygen and takes away waste products at a greater speed, creating a better environment for more effective soft tissue healing.

■ Lymph flow is greatly increased during and after massage treatment. During a

Right: athletes and sportspeople who train at a high level use massage to treat a range of sports injuries.

Increased confidence

Many massage practitioners claim that people treated with body massage become more positive and start enjoying their lives. They become more cheerful, less resentful and more understanding towards other people's problems. Their confidence comes back, and their wish to socialize again after a period of sometimes self-imposed isolation becomes apparent after only a few treatments. Depression and anxiety seem to disappear and their mental equilibrium recovers fully.

There is plenty of anecdotal evidence to illustrate this, but the results have not been put through rigorous scientific rules of research methodology. However, what we do know is that with the increased level of oxygen and more thorough and regular breathing, the functioning of the cardiovascular system becomes much more efficient. This, in turn, puts the body in an advantageous position for self-healing to take place because it can set time aside for this, and a sufficient level of the released resources can facilitate it.

thorough 'spring cleaning' of the body, the toxins can be more readily excreted. This takes place not only in terms of increased frequency of excretion and the quantity of waste products, but also in terms of quality of this 'spring cleaning' exercise, which promotes healthy regeneration of the damaged soft tissue as well as the internal organs.

This type of chain reaction is important in understanding the complexity of action that massage has on the body in its three-dimensional existence. People suffering from fluid retention benefit two-fold from massage treatment. They reduce their weight, which is good news for slimmers, but also they lose a substantial amount of fluid after the treatment. Fluid weighs on the same par as the adipose tissue or the muscle bulk in our bodies. Surplus fluid becomes a surplus weight in a body ridden with fluid retention; hence loss of fluid equals loss of weight.

Psychological effects

Physiologically, the body responds to massage treatment via the medium of physical touch and its effect on our physiological functions. However, it is the psychological effect of massage that always surprises me. People treated with body massage therapy respond very favourably with purely mental changes which take place afterwards. They often feel more relaxed and self-composed.

Often massage therapists listen to people's innermost secrets, pouring out from the darkness of the mind, having been bottled up for so long and now released; suddenly the mind is free from the burden. The release of mental tension is extremely beneficial and if this effect can be achieved by the application of body massage, then what other reactions can we expect from the body in response to massage therapy?

TOUCH IS HEALING IN ITSELF

Touch can be reassuring, caring or even violent, in which case the responses would be different to the ones described above. However, gentle and purposeful touch is soothing and therefore relaxing for the body, the mind and the spirit. Every human being operates on all these three levels, which are common to us all.

MASSAGE IN EVERYDAY LIFE

Massage therapy should be received on a regular basis. It should be regarded as a preventative therapy rather than a cure, and should be applied in order to maintain good health and well-being rather than to treat a particular complaint which has already afflicted the body. Stress is an ongoing occurrence in everyday life and hence we should use massage frequently to help prevent or minimize it.

A new influx of energy provides a good basis for mental stamina and physical fitness. Good health and well-being are attributes without which our mental and spiritual entities cannot exist. Oscar Firkins described it so cleverly when he wrote in his memoirs: 'Interest is a good, though loose, measure of well-being; in sickness everything is stupid for us but our pain'.

Below: massage can be used every day to combat stress at home and at work and to make people feel more relaxed.

CONTRAINDICATIONS TO BODY MASSAGE

Before learning the principles of massage, you need to acquaint yourself with certain conditions which are contraindications to body massage. Some of the common contraindications to massage are listed below.

■ Body massage is performed on the skin surface, and therefore the condition of the skin is of the utmost importance when assessing suitability for this type of tactile treatment.

■ Infectious skin diseases would preclude the treatment altogether, whereas areas of local skin inflammation or varicose veins could be avoided during a body massage session and only the surrounding area worked upon.

IT'S A MYSTERY!

Before you start your massage session, study the following quotation from Steven Mackenna in his Journal and Letters.
'The body is the mystery we know nothing of; it works its own will and goes its own way, like a cat or a god; as far as we know or have the power over it, its joy springs from the secrets of its own dark life, it dies by its own calendar, and when we most think we are ruling it, it is obeying the order itself first gave. It is the stranger; we can only gape at it when it stands in our doorway, and do our best to keep it in good humour, the awesome, powerful, venerable stranger.'

■ A very thin, dry, cracked and chapped skin would not lend itself to massage treatment, and conditions such as eczema, recent scar tissue, psoriasis and dermatitis would need to be assessed with great care before treatment.

■ People with very sensitive skin, which tends to go red upon even gentle rubbing, should not be vigorously massaged – to avoid the disappointment of no massage at all, they can be massaged with gentle stroking, feathering, superficial effleurage and very gentle kneading.

■ All cases of acute inflammation should be avoided. However, the massage treatment could be performed either above or below the affected areas, if it is at all realistic and possible.

■ A skin rash area should not be massaged at all. Friction on rubbing the skin may aggravate the skin condition, inflame it further and then cause the rash to spread, affecting an even greater area of skin.

■ A high fever and a raised body temperature are not the ideal circumstances in which to perform massage. This is because massage raises body temperature and increases its physiological activities, i.e. blood and lymph flow, excretion of toxins, etc. When the body systems are fighting off the infection this manifests itself in increased body temperature. The body's resources are tied up in this activity and hence there is usually very little surplus left to be

BODY AWARENESS

Rollo May said that the ability to be aware of one's body has a great importance all through life. It is a curious fact that most adults have lost their physical awareness to such an extent that they are unable to tell how their leg feels if you should ask them, or their ankle, or their middle finger or any other part of the body. He maintains that in our society the awareness of the different parts of the body is generally very limited. We can successfully resuscitate this awareness by the frequent use of therapeutic body massage.

channelled towards 'everyday' activities in the body's ordinary state of physiological functioning.

■ Cancer cases should be attended to with light pressure and a relaxing massage technique. Percussion should always be avoided altogether.

■ Gouty conditions are swollen and painful and this state of dysfunction in the body would preclude massage – it would be unpleasant and uncomfortable to the recipient of this treatment.

■ High blood pressure does not lend itself to body massage treatment and nor do cardiovascular conditions, such as thrombosis, phlebitis and angina pectoris. Friction, percussion and even kneading should be avoided at all costs as, if performed, they may cause more damage to the body.

■ Massage is also contraindicated in pregnancy, particularly unstable pregnancy, and painful or profuse menstruation.

■ The more specific contraindications relating to the strokes of tapotement and petrissage would apply also to cases of paralysed muscles, and joints or exposed areas of bone.

■ People who are suffering from nervous tension should not be massaged using the massage techniques incorporating petrissage and tapotement.

■ Diabetic patients should not be massaged, as a general rule. The skin tends to be very thin and there is a tendency to deep bruising. Vigorous massage is also contraindicated in this instance.

Below: there are some simple massage techniques, described later in the book, which you can perform on yourself at home.

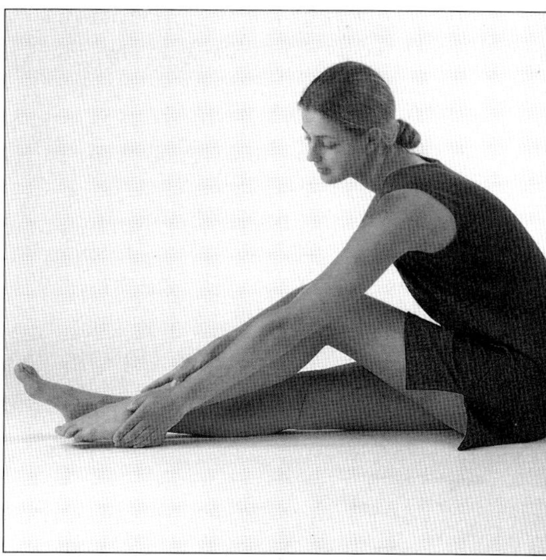

CHAPTER TWO

CARRIERS AND LUBRICANTS

Massage therapy has to be performed using a lubricant or some other medium in order to avoid friction. There is nothing more unpleasant than rubbing the skin too hard, which may cause irritation. Soft tissue manipulation should be applied with some cream, oil, balm or even talcum powder. The choice of medium for body massage may be left either to the therapist or the recipient. Judgmental factors may relate to the texture, temperature and age of the skin to be worked on, but generally a carrier oil of vegetable origin is used.

Below: natural vegetable oils are used as carrier oils for the essential oils.

CARRIER OILS

These form part of a general group known as 'fixed oils'. Vegetable carrier oils permeate through the skin with ease and are readily absorbed without leaving the skin greasy after treatment. The vegetable carrier oils that are most suitable for use in body massage are as follows:

- Sweet almond oil
- Apricot kernel oil
- Grapeseed oil
- Sesame seed oil

Richer oils, such as wheatgerm oil, particularly cold-pressed, are a natural antioxidant when mixed with other types of massage oils. Wheatgerm oil is excellent for dry and wrinkled skin.

Vitamin E is a very well-known skin regenerator, and, indeed, any other carrier oil containing vitamin E lends itself for treatment on a dry skin. Avocado oil is also very nourishing to the skin.

It is common practice to add only a proportion of these oils to the prepared blend for massage, say, five to ten per cent of wheatgerm oil, or, at the opposite end of the scale, ninety to ninety-five per cent of grapeseed oil. Avocado oil can be used on its own because it penetrates the skin quickly and is an added boon to treatment of lung conditions, obesity, fluid retention, cellulite and headaches.

SWEET ALMOND OIL

This oil is easily absorbed and gentle to the skin. It blends well with all the pure essential oils used in aromatherapy massage and is excellent for dry skin. Sweet almond oil is very safe to use, with a good texture and not too greasy. However, a word of warning: people who are allergic to almonds may react unfavourably to this carrier oil.

APRICOT KERNEL OIL

A very good facial oil, this is extremely nourishing and rich in unsaturated fatty acids and vitamins A and C. It is used in aromatherapy for facial treatments on normal and greasy skins.

COMFREY OIL

This is usually an infused carrier oil. It is unsurpassable as a soft tissue healer and rich in allantoin. Comfrey oil is particularly effective in therapeutic or remedial massage treatment where muscular aches and painful joints are the predominant features.

GRAPESEED OIL

This carrier oil is a very good 'all-rounder'. Not only is it nourishing for normal skin but it is also ideal for dry, rough skin. Grapeseed oil is rich in linoleic acid and hence it is very suitable for body massage treatment on people who wish to lose weight.

HAZELNUT OIL

Astringent in character, this carrier oil has specific applications for gouty conditions and swelling.

Above: there are many aromatherapy products for skincare and bathing.

Peach kernel oil

This oil is very suitable for dry, sensitive skin. It is used widely in aromatherapy facial treatments since its texture is thinner than that of any other carrier oils. Almost odourless, it enhances the aroma of essential oils and permeates easily through the skin.

Safflower oil

Cold-pressed safflower oil has many natural nourishing properties for tired and ageing skin. It is a well-proven skin rejuvenator.

Sesame seed oil

A good carrier oil for skin care, this is suitable for all skin types. If mixed with carrot oil, it preserves the elasticity of the skin.

Talcum powder

Talcs are excellent dry lubricants used for massaging small areas and ideal in situations where another medium is not convenient, e.g. on the neck and shoulder area. Non-perfumed talc is preferable because synthetic perfumes in the powder can irritate the skin. However, it should not be used on a hairy surface as it may irritate the hair follicles and cause the skin to itch. Also, it may enter the nostrils, causing sneezing and redness of the eyes.

Creams

These can be used for massage but are not suitable for hairy surfaces. Only creams with a simple natural base should be used as those containing synthetic perfumes may cause skin irritation and even an allergic reaction with redness and itching.

ESSENTIAL OILS

To help you choose a suitable essential oil for a specific treatment, some of the most important oils are listed below, together with an explanation of their beneficial action on the body. In fact, you can enrich your massage by the right choice of essential oil. Their specific action, in some cases, can enhance the benefits of treatment, both to the recipient and the giver alike.

Note: some pure essential oils should be used with care, and these oils have a note explaining the area of restricted application.

BASIL

An excellent nerve tonic. Basil strengthens concentration and clears the mind. It is a powerful insect repellent.

BENZOIN

Penetrating, warming and energizing for the heart. It is used for chapped and cracked skin, and as an inhalation for colds and laryngitis.

BERGAMOT

Uplifting, powerful anti-depressant and nerve sedative. It is good for treating cystitis and acne, and as an inhalation for lung conditions. Bergamot increases photosensitivity and it is therefore used in sun-tan preparations.

Caution: do not use immediately before prolonged exposure to sunlight.

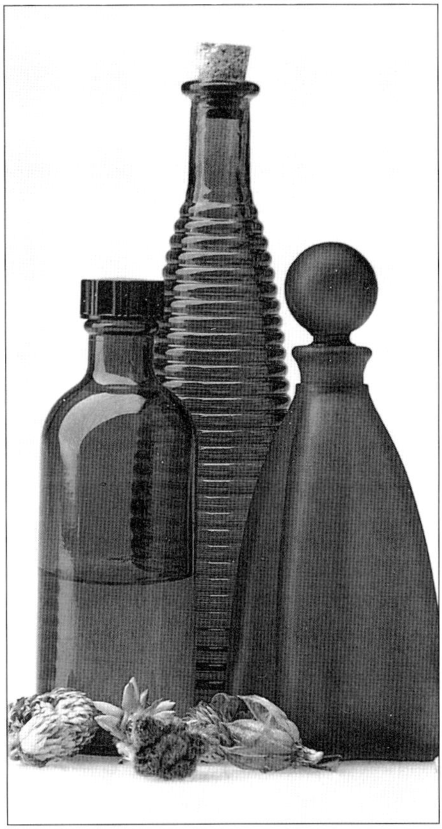

Above: essential oils are stored in dark bottles in a cool, dry place.

BLACK PEPPER

Warming, good for muscular aches and pains. It is used to increase circulation. It is the 'fiery' essential oil as it acts very quickly and creates drastic changes in status quo situations in the body. It helps treat the symptoms of colds and influenza, but is best used on the large joint areas.

CAJAPUT
Good for asthma, bronchitis and most respiratory disorders. It is also used in the treatment of laryngitis.

CEDARWOOD
Good for oily skin and acne. It is used in inhalations for lung conditions.
Caution: use with care during pregnancy.

CHAMOMILE
Anti-inflammatory and anti-allergic. Soothing and calming, this oil can relieve muscular aches and is good for treating insomnia. It is also a renowned remedy for teething discomfort.

CLARY SAGE
A very powerful relaxant. Clary Sage is excellent for people with insomnia, sore throats and laryngitis (as a gargle).
Caution: it clashes with alcohol during treatment.

CYPRESS
Excellent for heavy menstruation and helps clear varicose veins. This oil is used in inhalations for influenza and coughs.

EUCALYPTUS
An antiseptic and anti-viral agent. It is an excellent insect repellent. Eucalyptus is used as an inhalation when treating asthma, bronchitis and sinusitis.

FENNEL
A carminative and digestive remedy. Fennel oil is also used in treating cellulite.

GERANIUM
Excellent for throat and mouth infections, eczema, ulcers and dermatitis. This essential oil is a 'general cleanser' and cleanses as it goes along, be it the skin, digestive system, mouth cavity or the excretory system.

GRAPEFRUIT
A light, uplifting citrus oil of aphrodisiac quality. It is an effective remedy for cellulite and fluid retention. This essential oil is a 'sunny oil' because its uplifting

Left: Chamomile.

properties are very strong and it has a pronounced effect on depressed individuals with a tendency towards dullness and slowness of mind.

JASMINE

The king of oils. One of the most exquisite of scents, Jasmine is a uterine tonic and strong sensual stimulant. It is invaluable for treating symptoms with a psychological or psychosomatic origin (e.g. apathy, depression and insomnia).

JATAMANSI

Excellent for painful muscles and joints, arthritis and insomnia. This oil possesses strong anti-inflammatory and relaxing properties. A hair stimulant and dark hair colour restorer for grey hair, it is used widely for this purpose by Tibetan herbalists.

JUNIPER BERRY

A refreshing and invigorating agent. This oil successfully remedies cellulite and fluid retention in the body. It is also used as a remedy for skin disorders (oily skin and acne) and gout.

LAVENDER

A heart tonic and nerve sedative of normalizing, analgesic and antiseptic action. It is excellent for aches and pains, and may be added to bath water or used in massage oil. For migraines and headaches, apply a drop to the temples, or use in a cold compress. The description of a good 'all-rounder' applies to Lavender very well.

LEMON

Used in gargling for sore throats and in treating insect bites and stings. Use neat on warts and veruccas. To stop bleeding, dab Lemon oil on small cuts in a two per cent solution in boiled water.

LEMONGRASS

An invigorating oil for use in the bath and in body massage. It is a cleanser for oily skin (acne) and a renowned gastric stimulant.

LIME

Contains vitamin C. It is a strong astringent with multiple culinary uses. It also remedies diarrhoea and digestive disorders.

MANDARIN

A refreshing citrus oil. It has relaxing and uplifting characteristics but not on as high a level as Grapefruit.

MARIGOLD

An excellent remedy for healing and for renewing body tissue. It is used to treat chilblains, remedies inflammation and heals bruises and burns.

MARJORAM

Anti-spasmodic, warming for the muscles and heart. Marjoram reduces menstrual pain and anxiety. It is a good remedy for insomnia and muscular discomfort.

MELISSA

Rejuvenating with some anti-depressant properties. It is used for allergies, tension

and heart problems. It is also excellent for bee and wasp stings.
Caution: if used in greater quantity, it can become a skin desensitizer.

MYRRH
A cooling anti-inflammatory oil with rejuvenating properties.

NEROLI (ORANGE BLOSSOM)
The most effective oil for treating anxiety, hysteria, depression and palpitations. Neroli is also an excellent remedy for shock and fear. It is especially good for dry skin, broken capillaries and veins. Neroli oil is an exquisite, intoxicating scent, and very economical in use; it can be used as a perfume or added to toilet waters.

NIAOULI
Good for respiratory conditions and also urinary infections.

ORANGE
High vitamin C content. Orange is an effective remedy for insomnia, diarrhoea, palpitations, dry skin, and broken capillaries. Since this is a citrus oil, it acts as an uplifting and rejuvenating essential oil.

PATCHOULI
Renowned as an aphrodisiac, Patchouli is a musky, sweet and sensual oil. A powerful stimulant, it lifts states of anxiety and depression. Patchouli promotes formation of scar tissue and is suitable for mature skin, dryness and inflammation.

PEPPERMINT
Remedies digestive disorders and nausea. This oil alleviates travel sickness and migraine. It is a powerful insect repellent and has definite cooling characteristics.

PETITGRAIN
A wonderfully relaxing oil. Petitgrain is very suitable for acne.

PINE
An excellent remedy for all infections of the respiratory tract (inhalation), gout and rheumatism.

ROSE
A beautiful feminine scent with a tenacious aroma. Rose is one of the most antiseptic essences and the least toxic essential oil. A powerful anti-depressant, it soothes the nerves and hence it is the best remedy for treating disorders of the female reproductive system. In skin care, it is good for dry, mature and sensitive skin.

ROSEMARY
Stimulates memory and hair growth, and invigorates circulation. It is also good for dandruff and very effective for vertigo and dullness.
Caution: Rosemary is a stimulating oil and therefore is not very suitable for people with high blood pressure.

ROSEWOOD
A light, subtle aroma. It is very good for sensitive skin and for relaxation. It has a

Above: Sage and Rosemary (right).

pronounced effect on the emotional level, helping to restore imbalances in the mind.

SAGE
Relieves labour pains and combats obesity. It is a good nerve tonic and counteracts swelling. Sage is astringent in action.

SANDALWOOD
Useful in states of anxiety and nervous tension. A sweet, woody scent, it evokes a meditative atmosphere. Sandalwood treats chronic infections within the genito-urinary and pulmonary tracts. As well as being very good for dry skin and acne, it is a powerful aphrodisiac.

SUGANDHA KOKILA
Used to treat ailments of the digestive system, e.g. flatulence and diarrhoea. It is good for rheumatism, joint pain and muscular aches.

TEA TREE
A powerful antiseptic. This oil is effective in action for cuts, infections and colds.

THYME
A powerful antiseptic. Used in bath oil, Thyme can relieve muscular pain.

XANTHOXYLUM
Has a stimulating effect on the lymphatic and circulatory systems as well as the mucus membranes.

CREATING THE RIGHT ENVIRONMENT

Now that you have a much better understanding of body massage and the carrier and essential oils that are used, you are ready to start preparing for this new and wonderful experience. One of the most important things to remember is the comfort of the person being massaged.

STAYING WARM

Make sure that the temperature of the room in which the treatment will take place is sufficient for the person being massaged to relax when undressed. Make it more pleasant by supplying some warm towels to cover the body during treatment.

BEDS AND COUCHES

You may choose to give the recipient a massage on a bed. If you can get access to the body from both sides and it is not too low for you, a bed is very convenient for body massage. However, if you can afford a couch, this is even better as it will be more accessible and a more suitable height.

A RELAXING ENVIRONMENT

If you like relaxing music, put on some quiet background music which will have a calming effect on both of you. See to these details before you start the massage treatment. You can create a soothing and

USE QUALITY OILS

The quality of the pure essential oils used for body massage treatment is paramount. Always choose high-quality oils from a reputable source. Synthetic oils, which are readily available, are not suitable for body massage treatment; they may cause irritation, itching and even trigger off an allergic reaction. You should always try to enhance your body massage with the most beautiful natural aromas of the highest quality so that you can benefit from the treatment as well as the person you are massaging.

The body remembers past pleasures and, when induced to reminisce, it floods the mind with sweet memories. Pure essential oils, once remembered, will always trigger off the most pleasurable of thoughts and memories with each application.

fragrant aroma by using essential oils in a burner or on a tissue placed on a radiator, on a pillow, or even in the blend of massage oils prepared for treatment.

LIGHTING

The lighting should not be too bright nor from a central point on the ceiling. A dimmed light from a side wall, or even a bedside table, is preferable. Shaded and romantic, the light should accentuate the relaxed atmosphere. The pleasurable anticipation of the imminent massage can be highlighted by minute details, such as positioning the pillow correctly on the couch and covering the body with a towel during treatment.

MASSAGE CHECKLIST

You need to check the following things before commencing the massage.

■ Make sure that you have short nails so that you will not scratch the person being massaged. Not only is this unpleasant and painful but it can also leave visible signs of your fingers on sensitive skin at the end of the treatment.

■ You need to be relaxed and really comfortable. If your hair is long or tends to fall forwards over your face, it should be tied back so that you will not have to interrupt the flow of the sequence by having to push it back out of your eyes, or even by trying to prevent long hair touching the body on the couch.

■ If you are using pure essential oils, ensure that you are not wearing a scent which would clash unfavourably with the aroma of the oil.

■ As for the person being massaged, provide some warm towels and a warm environment as well as subtle lighting to help induce relaxation.

■ Above all, you must develop a good rapport between you. If the body massage is to be beneficial, you both need to be in harmony.

CALMING THE MIND

Dr Dowse, an eminent Victorian physician, remarked in 1887: 'The mind, which before massage is in a perturbed, restless, vacillating and even despondent state, becomes, after massage, calm, quiet, peaceful and subdued; in fact the wearied and worried mind has been converted into a mind restful, placid, and refreshed.'

COMBATING STRESS

Stress is a killer. Indeed, it may be responsible for seventy-five per cent of all diseases in the Western world. Although stress is not a new occurrence, its far-reaching consequences are frightening in their magnitude. It affects not only the mind, but also the physical body and the spiritual life of all of us. Massage is one of the natural methods helping to eradicate the symptoms of stress. It can play an active and positive role in stress management.

MASSAGE TECHNIQUES

There are several massage strokes which are commonly used in body massage. They can be performed at different speeds, with variable frequency and individually chosen or preferred pressure. It is important to learn the basic massage strokes before embarking on an experimental expedition of this type of treatment.

Below: this photograph shows the correct positioning of the hands to start neck and shoulders effleurage.

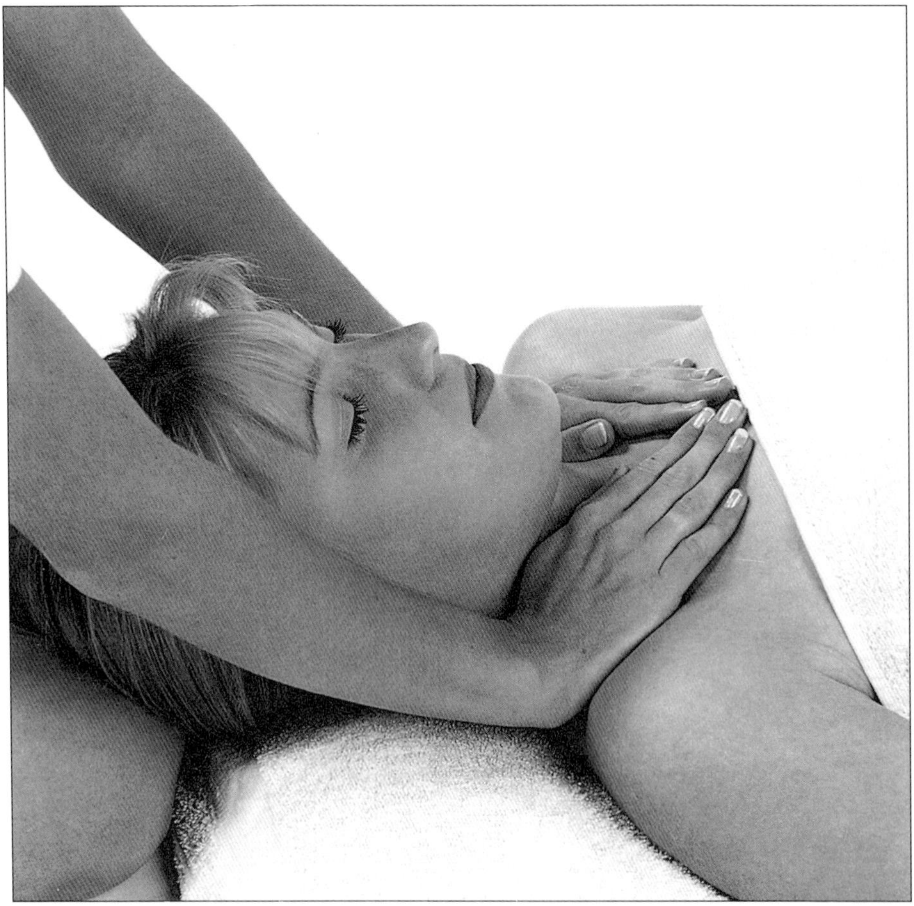

EFFLEURAGE

This movement is the most common stroke used in body massage. It is performed with the flat of the hand (palms and fingers) over a large area, or the pads of the fingers (as opposed to the fingertips) over a small area. This stroke precedes all other movements in body massage because it has a very relaxing effect.

- It enables the recipient to get used to the temperature and skin texture of the therapist's hands.
- It enables the therapist to apply the medium or lubricant, such as a good-quality vegetable oil, on the surface of the person's skin to be massaged.

BENEFITS OF EFFLEURAGE

Effleurage improves venous flow, relieves congestion and increases the excretion of waste products. It also speeds up the lymphatic circulation. Effleurage is very soothing, allowing the recipient to relax. Deeper effleurage is useful in treating sprains; superficial effleurage hastens healing in cases such as fractures.

Below: in effleurage, as here on the neck in a prone position, the hands are always in contact with the body.

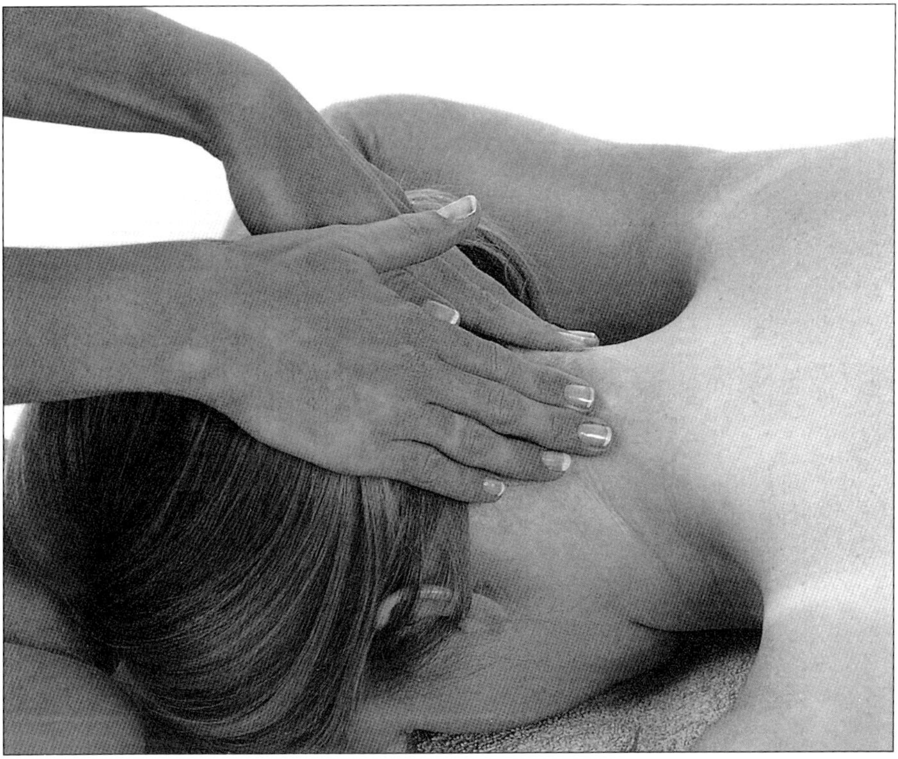

■ This movement is usually introduced in between other strokes in body massage. One of the most popular strokes, it is easy to learn and its application is almost 'universal' in massage.

Effleurage can be performed as a superficial stroke – always in the return direction from deep stroking. However, it can also be used as a deep stroke – performed with pressure in the direction of the heart – because it helps the venous flow and as such can be used on its own. In fact, effleurage is sometimes called 'stroking'.

THE TECHNIQUE

■ When applying effleurage, the hands should be relaxed from the wrists and in contact with the body all the time, moulding themselves round the part to be treated.

■ On their return, allow them to glide gently over the skin. If a particular area of the body requires stimulation, a succession of quick effleurage movements could be introduced.

■ The technique of effleurage movement is very easy to learn because to stroke either lightly or with slight pressure is almost instinctive for any human being. The most convenient area on which to learn this stroke is the back: the torso and the buttocks.

Opposite: this is the starting position for neck effleurage with the person to be massaged lying face-down, their head supported on a pillow or cushion for comfort. Effleurage is a very soothing stroke if performed properly.

USING THE FINGERTIPS

The idea of body massage is to cover as large an area of the body as possible in order to make the treatment beneficial and pleasurable. Hence the whole of the flat of the hands should be used in this stroke (particularly so if the hands are small and belong to a petite owner).

SUMMARY

Now that the oil has been applied to the whole surface of the skin and you feel the rhythm of the movement is relaxing for you and the recipient, another stroke can be introduced into the sequence. Approach the next step of learning with confidence and fulfilled expectations.

KEY POINTS

In order to improve the quality of the movement, you should remember to avoid the following:

■ Jerky strokes: continuous movement should be maintained at all times.

■ Losing contact with the body on the lighter return movement: loss of contact spoils the relaxation and fluency of the massage stroke.

■ Hairy surfaces: if the legs or chest area are covered with hair, more lubricant can be used to prevent friction. It will facilitate continuity of strokes as well as fluency of the technique used between different strokes.

EFFLEURAGE IN BACK MASSAGE

Effleurage is used as a first stroke in order to apply the oil on the skin.

1 Place some oil on the palms of your hands and then place both hands at the bottom of the spine with the tips of the fingers facing upward and glide slowly in an upward direction. Some pressure may be introduced here – as much as you feel appropriate.

2 It is a long movement and when you have reached the top of the shoulders, part the hands to the side and slide gently downwards on the sides of the ribcage.

3 This return movement should bear no pressure and your hands should meet at the small of the back again so that you can repeat the upward movement – this time with some pressure.

4 Part the hands at the top of the shoulders and come down gently, allowing your relaxed hands to rest on each side at the bottom of the spine.

5 Start again with a firm upward movement and then come down slowly with your hands on both sides of the torso back to your starting position. This stroke should be fluent and rhythmical and your hands should be continuously in contact with the recipient's body.

1

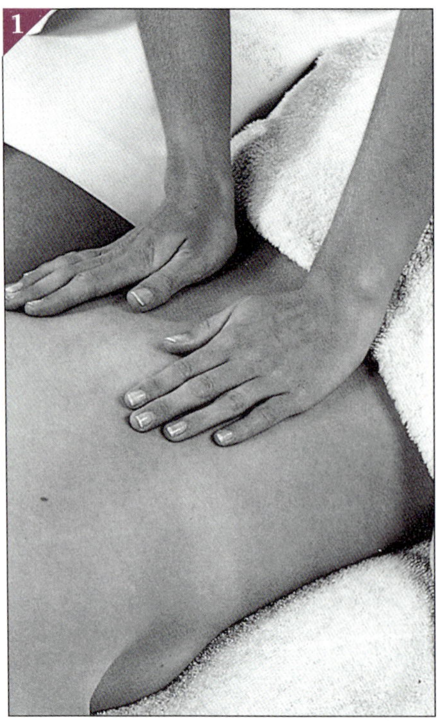

2

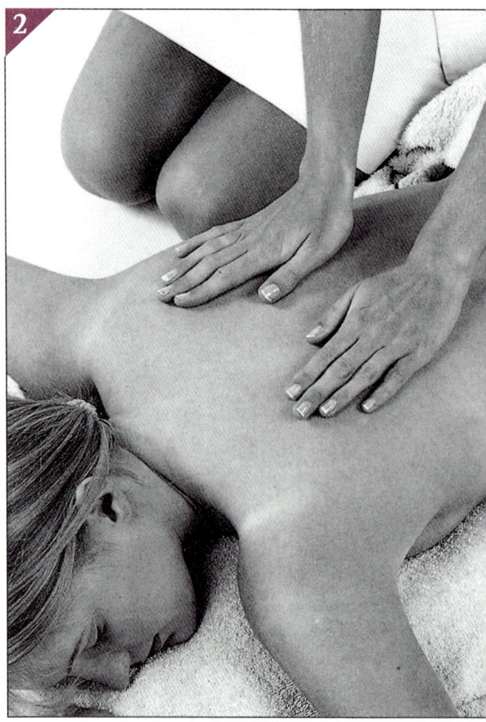

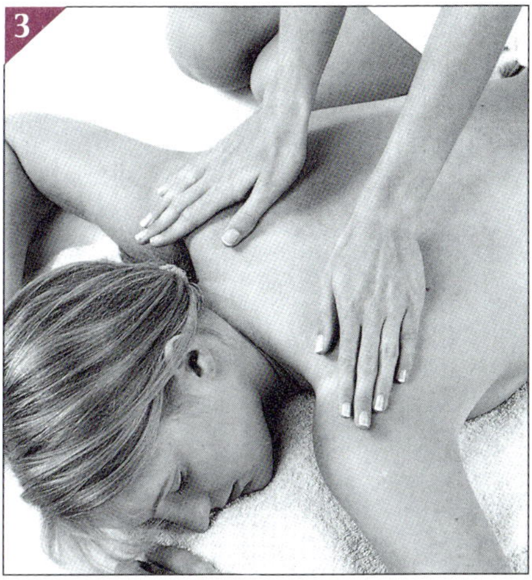
3

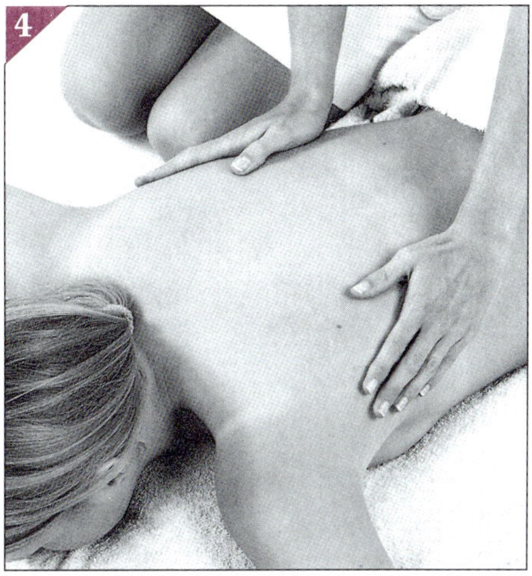
4

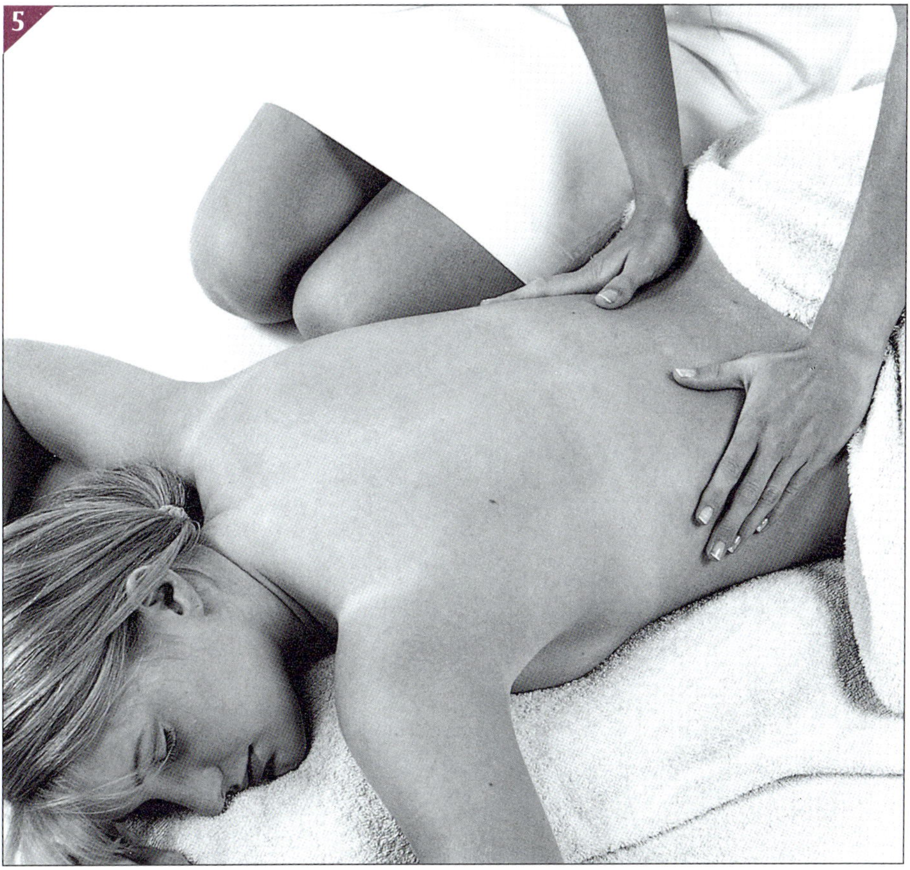
5

PETRISSAGE

Petrissage is usually applied with the balls of the fingers or thumbs to the muscle which lies directly over the bone, by applying pressure on the soft tissue by pressing the muscle against the bone.

THE TECHNIQUE

■ Petrissage should be performed with the cushions of the thumbs or the balls of the fingers in a sequence of circular movements. This type of deep rubbing in circles can be used on the wrists or the buttocks.

■ Petrissage is often used in facial

BENEFITS OF PETRISSAGE

Petrissage breaks down fatty and fibrous tissue as well as tension nodules. It brings a fresh and vigorous supply of blood to the part of the body being treated. This stroke aids the removal of excess fluid in the body and stimulates circulation.

Below: this shows petrissage, otherwise known as friction, to the shoulders in the prone position.

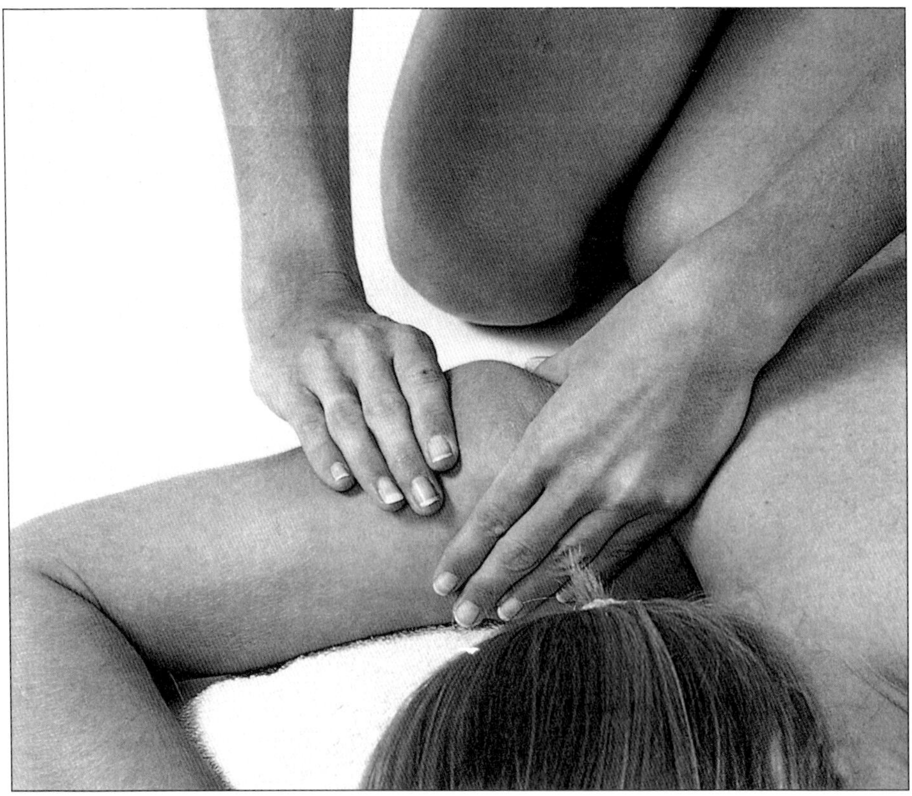

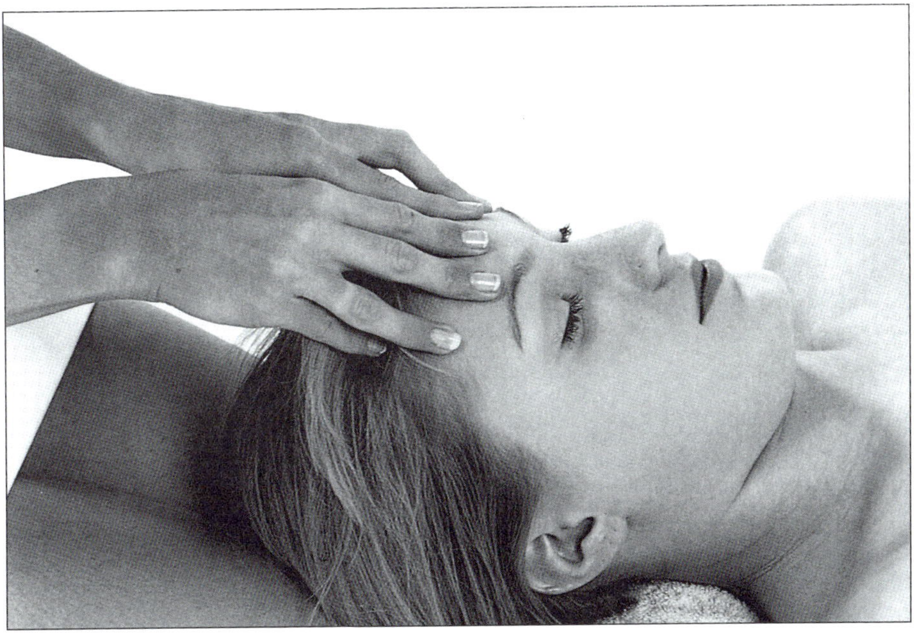

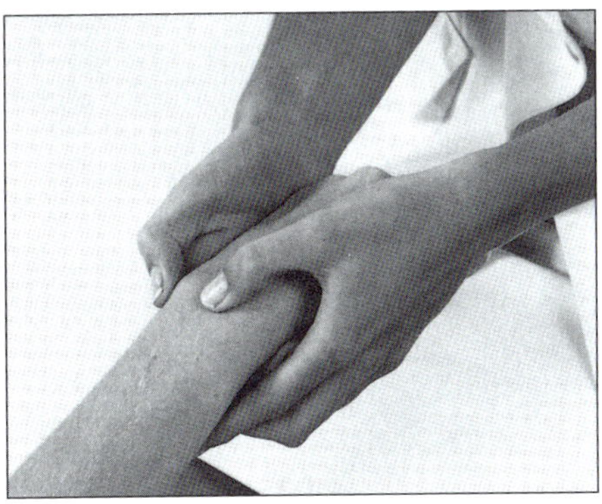

Above: here petrissage is being used on the forehead during a head massage. It is an invigorating stroke, aiding circulation and breaking down tension nodules.
Left: petrissage, with its deep circular motion, is a particularly suitable stroke for using on the wrists.

treatments on the forehead with light circular movements. The forehead is a small area and hence the stroke is performed with the fingertips as opposed to the balls of the fingers.

■ Pay special attention to the way this stroke is performed; it should not slide over the skin but should move the tissue over the bone.

KEY POINTS

When performing petrissage, you need to remember to avoid the following:

■ Inflamed areas of skin: rubbing can spread the inflammation.

■ Tender areas: the pressure of this stroke may become painful at these points.

■ Recent fractures or scar tissue: petrissage is not suitable for these conditions.

PETRISSAGE IN BACK MASSAGE

Petrissage movement may be introduced as a second stroke after effleurage and should be performed with the thumbs of both hands, parallel to, but on both sides of, the spine.

1 Press the muscles with both thumbs in small circles against the bone underneath (spinal vertebrae should part the thumbs).

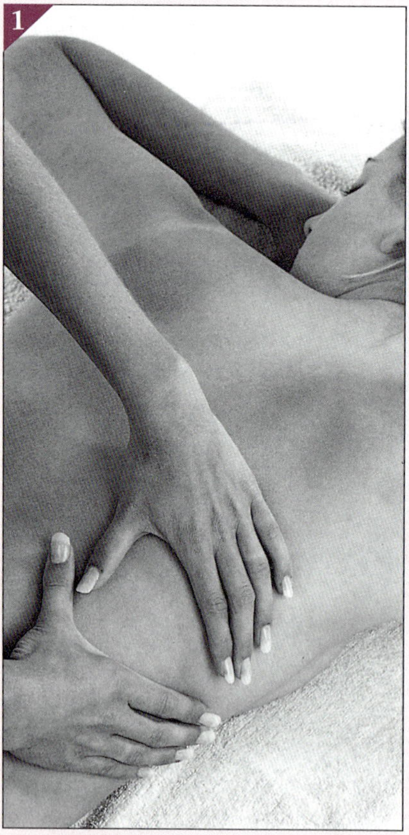

Each time, after repeated circles on the spot, move slightly upwards to start another circling sequence higher up the torso.

2 You may repeat the sequence once or twice and intersperse it with effleurage before you move your hands and perform petrissage on the buttocks area.

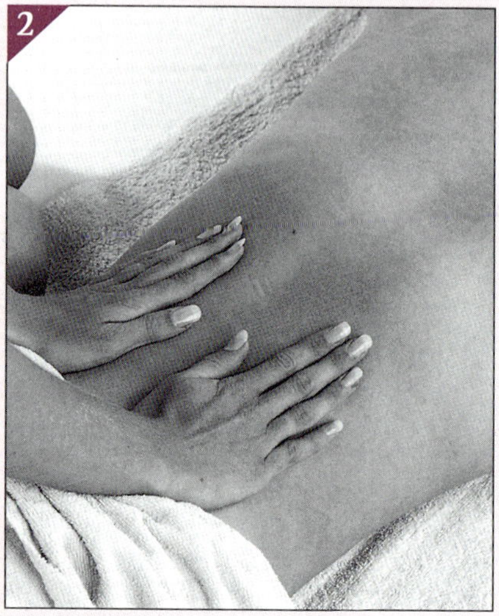

Note: If you apply it to the buttocks, in order to achieve deeper pressure, it is important to stiffen the elbows to press the thumbs more deeply. The soft tissue underneath needs to be trapped and worked on firmly in small circular movements, making sure that the fingers or the thumbs do not slide on the surface of the skin.

You can work this area starting from the bottom of the spine to the side, and on the repeated movement you can start 2.5cm (1in) lower. Proceed with some circular movements from the middle to the sides and on the last stroke cover the bottom part of the buttocks. Finish the session with some effleurage on the whole area of the back.

KNEADING

The third stage of learning body massage is now ready to be taken on board. This stroke is always favoured by body massage therapists and those who receive it alike. Kneading has a very profound and deep effect on the muscles and is usually performed on the soft tissue only – the muscles that have no bone surface underneath. Therefore, groups of muscles, such as the buttocks, top of the shoulders and around the waist area on the back of the body, would best lend themselves to this movement.

This stroke derives its name from an

BENEFITS OF KNEADING

The effects of kneading are numerous. It increases circulation and the removal of waste products. Superficial or 'surface' tissue is stimulated into further activity. The muscle tone is increased (a good stroke for slimmers) and kneading assists in preventing stiffness after vigorous exercise. It breaks down fatty and fibrous tissue. Deep kneading movements treat whole muscle groups and, therefore, they have a long-term effect of relaxing tight, tense and congested soft tissue in the body.

Below: deep kneading on the neck and shoulders helps to relax them.

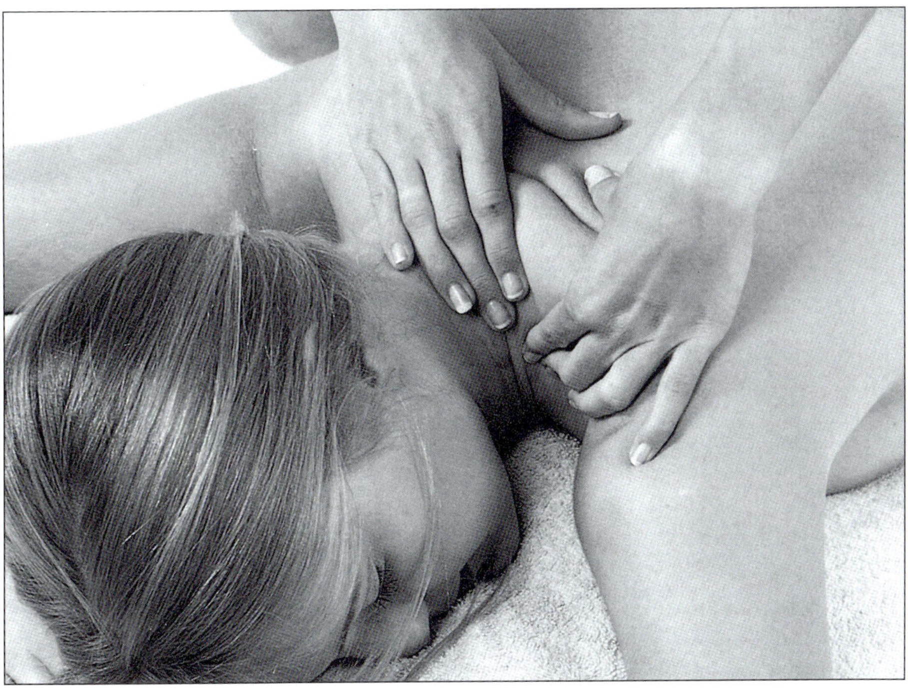

activity performed in the kitchen rather than on the couch. In body massage, the kneading stroke is performed in the same way as the action of kneading bread. The principle of the technique is very similar.

THE TECHNIQUE

- Imagine that you are kneading dough. Pick a muscle or a group of muscles and squeeze this bulk of flesh. The aim of this action is to pick it up away from the bone and squeeze it between the fingers and thumb of one hand. The fingers should be straight throughout the stroke.
- Then release the pressure whilst the other hand moves to the adjacent area to perform the movement again.
- This stroke is usually performed with the hands alternating, using the palm and whole length of the fingers, or the thumb and fingers, depending on the size of the muscle area being worked upon. You need to transfer the flesh from one hand to the other and handle it firmly between the thumb and the fingers.

KEY POINTS

When kneading, you must remember to avoid the following:

- Performing kneading as a first movement: it should always be preceded by effleurage.
- Nipping of the skin: this is very unpleasant and usually not tolerated well by the person undergoing treatment.
- Exerting too much pressure: adjust your pressure according to the pain tolerance of the recipient.

KNEADING IN BACK MASSAGE

1 Place both hands on top of the shoulders with the fingers facing each other and thumbs facing each other so that you have the bulk of the muscle in between the thumb and the fingers of each hand.

2 Move the right hand towards the left, squeezing and rolling the muscle, and move it away so that the left hand can move in and handle the flesh, moving towards the right.

3 Let go of the muscle bulk and retreat so that the right hand can take over now.

4 Once you observe that the colour of the flesh is changing to pink, you need to move on to the neighbouring area of muscle – this movement should be done without losing contact with the skin surface – and continue repeating the squeezing and rolling of the same area of flesh smoothly from one hand to the other as if you were kneading dough.

5 One hand releases the muscle and the other gathers it again, squeezing and rolling and letting the first hand pick the movement up. Continuity of movement is essential in this stroke. The movement has a feeling of waves going up and down, or gentle rocking from side to side. Attune your body to this stroke and enjoy it.

6 Slide both hands sideways and repeat the routine on the area of the buttocks.

7 Finish with effleurage on the whole area of the back.

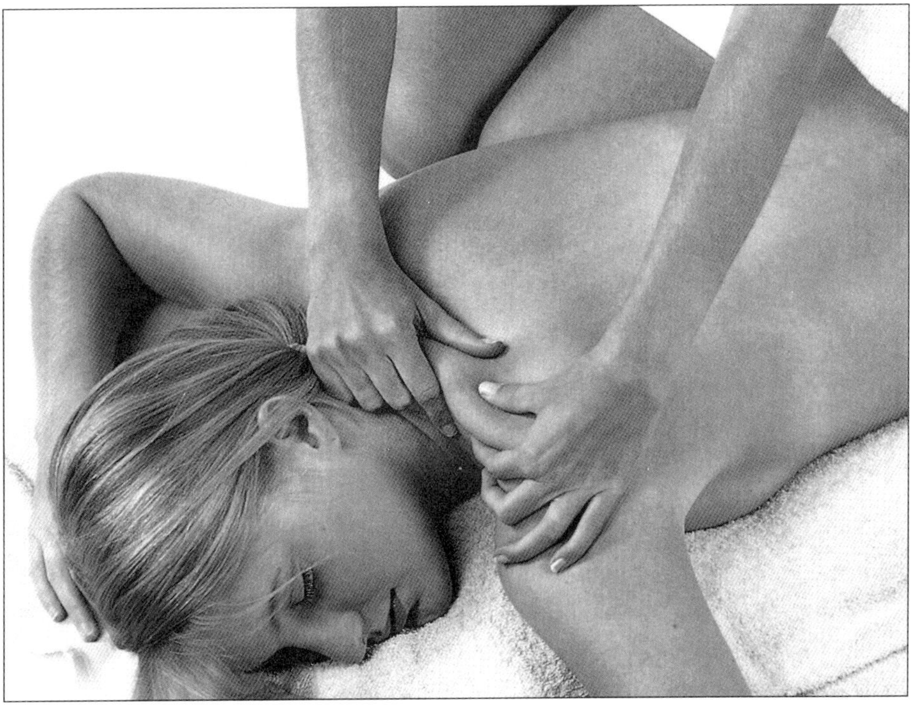

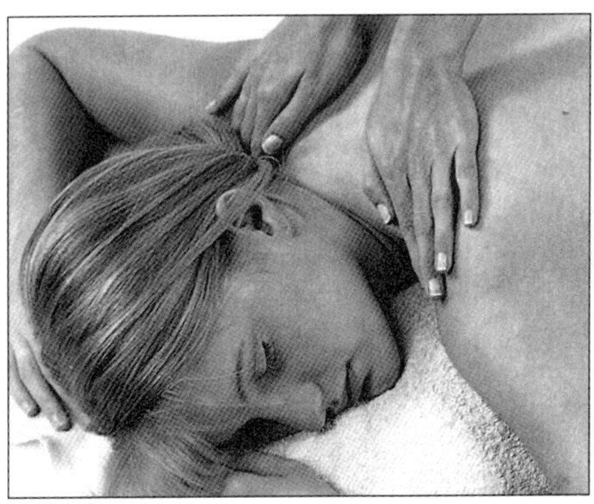

This photographic sequence shows a succession of deep kneading movements on the neck and shoulders areas. Make sure that you do not exert too much pressure or nip the skin; kneading should be enjoyable, not painful!

PERCUSSION

If you feel that you have succeeded in mastering the three basic movements of body massage described above, you are now ready to move on to the technique called percussion, which includes strokes bearing the names of hacking, cupping, pounding and plucking.

THE TECHNIQUES

1 HACKING

■ This is performed with the ulnar border of the hands and palms facing each other in a quick series of alternating movements up and down.

■ The fingers should be fairly relaxed and the success of this technique lies in the movement from the wrist, which should be

Below: the hacking technique is being used here on the backs of the legs.

BENEFITS OF PERCUSSION

Percussion has many beneficial effects on the psychological as well as on the physiological level. It manifests itself physically by the increased muscle tone and stimulated blood supply to the area being treated. The skin may appear slightly pink or even red, and the change of colour usually indicates an increased level of activities underneath. Percussion aids the breaking down of fatty tissues and also the removal of toxins by increasing lymph flow and stimulating blood circulation. Percussion is a stimulating massage technique; hence it has a similar effect on the psychological level. It stimulates a sluggish way of thinking and elevates the perception of touch via a stimulating effect on the nerve endings.

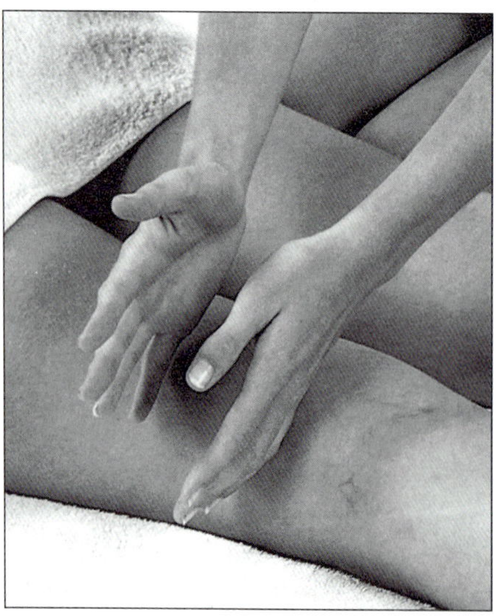

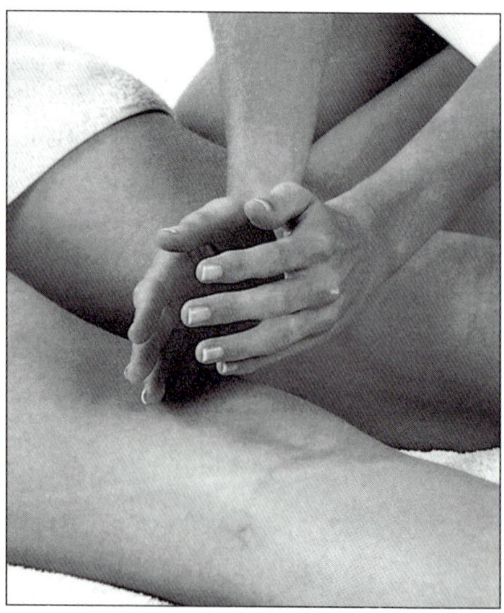

flexible at all times because it is this that dictates the movement.

■ You now need to develop the skill of alternating the 'up and down' movement of the hands so as not to lose contact with the body. The fingers should be working very quickly and whilst one hand is up, the other one should be touching the body.

■ This stroke requires a lot of patience and co-ordination for it to be effective and, at the same time, to be pleasant for the recipient of body massage.

2 Cupping

■ This involves both hands forming a hollow, with the fingers extended, in a succession of quick, speedy 'up and down' movements from the wrist. In effect, it is the hollow of the palm of the hands touching the flesh and it requires good rhythm and co-ordination.

■ The cupped hands should be arched at the knuckles and on coming down they should be able to 'trap' the air in an enclosed space between the arched hand and the flesh.

■ When the hand goes up, losing the contact, the trapped air is released, and when the air is expelled from the vacuum, it makes a loud noise. Meanwhile, the other hand should come down, trapping the air. The resulting suction brings the blood

Below: the correct position of the hands forming a hollow for the cupping stroke, with the fingers extended.

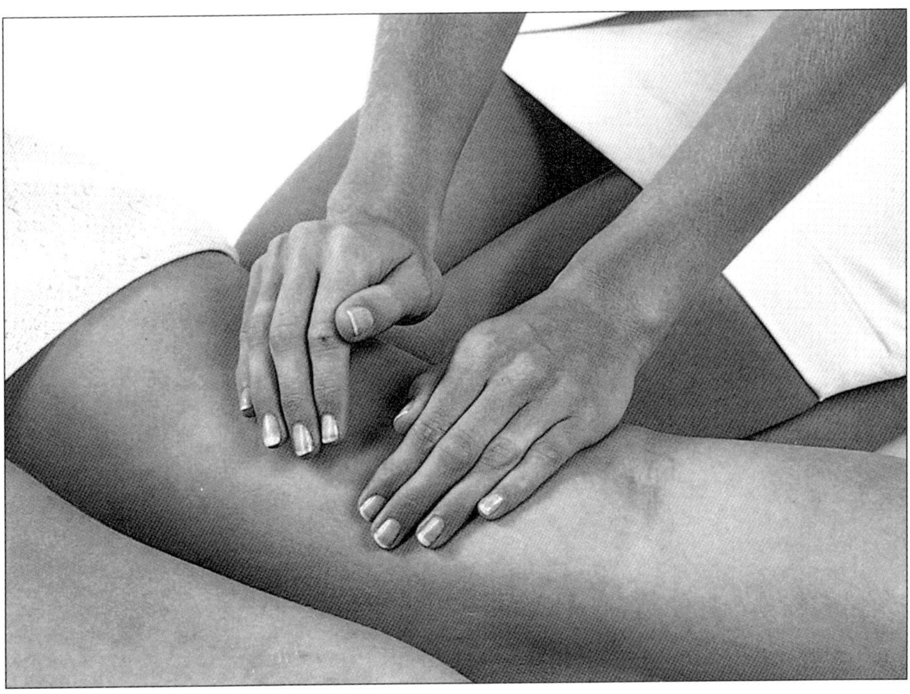

KEY POINTS

Percussion should not be performed in the following instances:

■ On a paralysed muscle: due to the absence of feedback and the affected nerve endings not receiving tactile stimuli as per the normal response level.

■ On bony areas, or where bones are covered by only a thin layer of muscle tissue and skin: percussion is not at all comfortable for the therapist and may be unpleasant for the recipient.

■ On sensitive areas of the body such as the abdomen: the close vicinity of the solar plexus would prevent the body relaxing during percussion.

■ On tender or painful areas: the strokes have impetus and are relatively quick and multiple in execution, instigating tenderness or causing aggravation to a painful area.

■ On a person of a nervous predisposition: percussion strokes are performed with a certain level of pressure and the severity of multiple impact with the skin and muscle underneath stimulates nerve endings, making the nervous system alert and working throughout the sequence.

■ During pregnancy: the achieved stimulation may be too spontaneous and may cause disturbance in the status quo of a pregnant woman. This contraindication would particularly apply in cases of unstable pregnancy.

to the surface and the skin changes to a slightly pink colour.

■ Cupping is also called clapping which should be distinguished from 'slapping'. Slapping is very unpleasant and should be avoided in body massage. However, skillfully performed hacking and cupping promote a vigorous flow of blood to the area and circulation is greatly improved, resulting in increased muscle tone. This is good news for people preparing themselves for strenuous exercise or for slimmers, who wish to improve their muscle tone to achieve a perfect figure and an improved body shape.

3 FLICKING OR PLUCKING

■ This is performed by using only the outstretched fingers to give a lighter movement. The flesh is handled between the thumbs and fingertips and should slip easily away between the fingers with each stroke.

■ The flesh should not be pinched since this will prevent the recipient from relaxing and may prove painful and unpleasant.

SUMMARY

■ **Hacking** is applied for the purpose of improving muscle tone. It is used predominantly on the back and legs, and lightly on the shoulder area. It increases blood supply to the larger muscles of the body and, by doing so, it helps to excrete toxins. It breaks down adipose tissue and prevents stiffness.

■ **Cupping** brings the blood supply to the surface of the skin. It is mainly performed

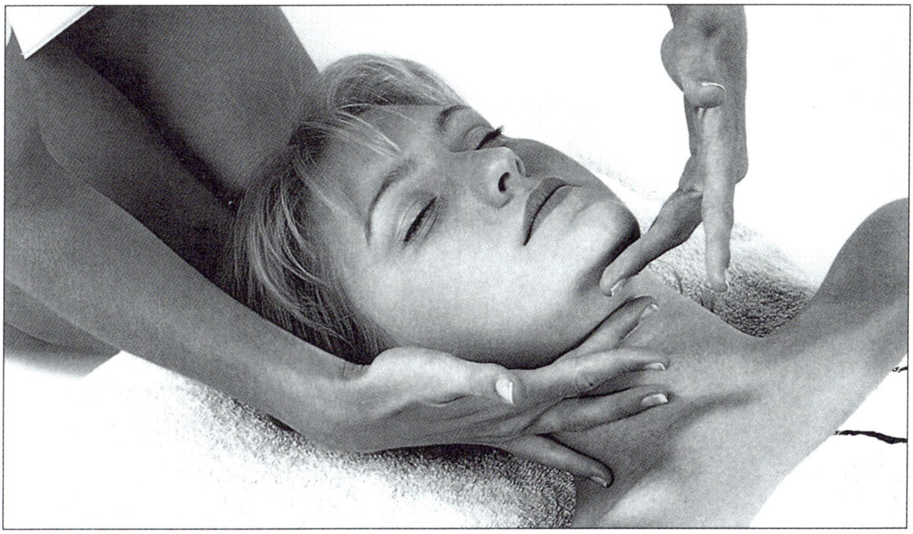

Above: flicking is a light, relaxing stroke in which the flesh is handled between thumbs and fingertips.

on the back, legs, sides of the abdomen and the top of the shoulders. This stroke has a toning-up effect on the soft tissue. It increases suppleness and prevents stiffening after exercise. Cupping has a very beneficial effect on the improved lymph flow and the renewal of waste products via increased blood flow in the area.

■ **Flicking,** or plucking, aids relaxation of the muscles, improves muscle tone and is well known for its rejuvenating effects on the nerve endings and the skin. Flicking stimulates blood circulation but instigates it in a relaxing and gentle way. This stroke can be used safely even on people suffering from nervous strain. It lends itself to being performed on fleshy parts of the body but the effect in psychological terms is of a relaxing nature, whereas in physiological terms, it is very stimulating.

PERCUSSION IN BACK MASSAGE

1 These movements are best performed starting from the buttocks area and moving upwards, very lightly over the ribcage and shoulder area, coming down on the other side of the lower back. Fluency of movement is essential and changing from one stroke to the other should be done without interrupting the flow of these strokes.

2 When finished, this sequence can be followed by some light effleurage.

FEATHERING

Now is the time to conclude the massage session by applying a gentle stroke, called feathering, which can be introduced at the end of a massage session.

THE TECHNIQUE

- You need to keep your arms and hands very relaxed. Simply brush the skin lightly with your fingertips starting from the top of the shoulders, one hand at a time, alternating your hands.
- Run your fingers slowly from the top to the bottom of the spine. Feathering is usually applied only on the back of the body.
- This stroke finishes the sequence and aids relaxation with its light, caring, delicate touch. When your hands meet at the bottom of the spine, draw the towel up in order to cover the area you have been

Below: this shows the feathering technique applied to the back.

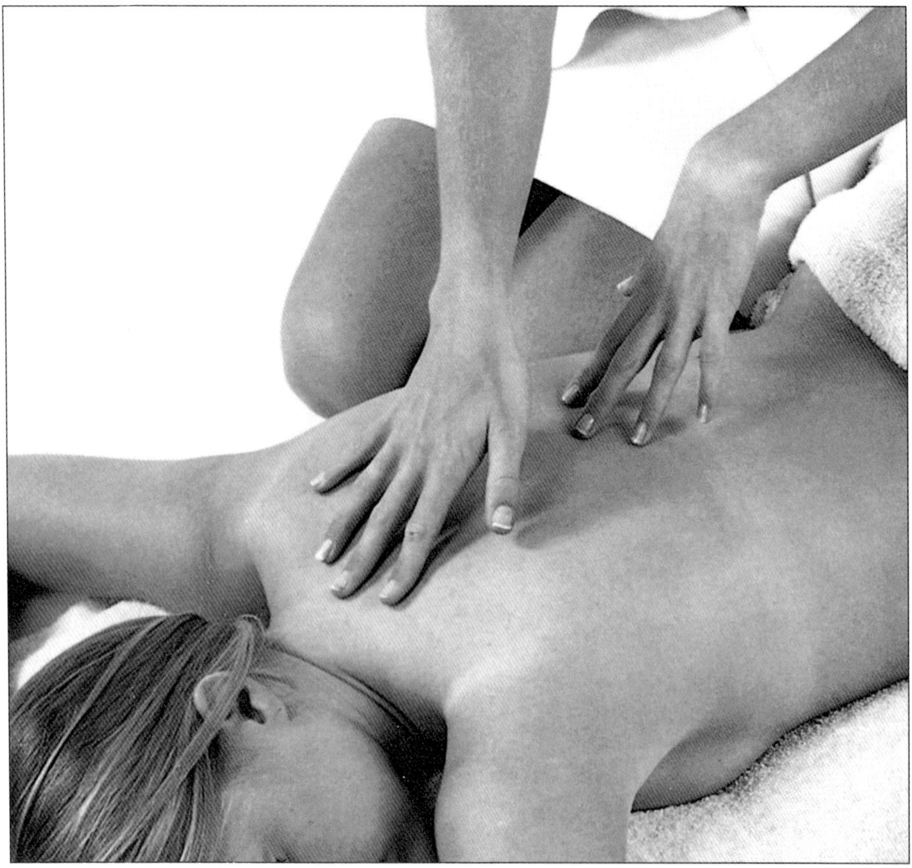

working on to keep it warm and free from any tension.

■ Then uncover one of the legs and proceed with the feathering technique you have acquired.

■ Do remember to apply effleurage in between strokes when the leg is being massaged. Afterwards, cover the leg with the towel and proceed to the other one so that the treatment of the back of the body may be concluded.

Right and below: effleurage is applied between the feathering strokes, as shown here on the back and backs of the legs.

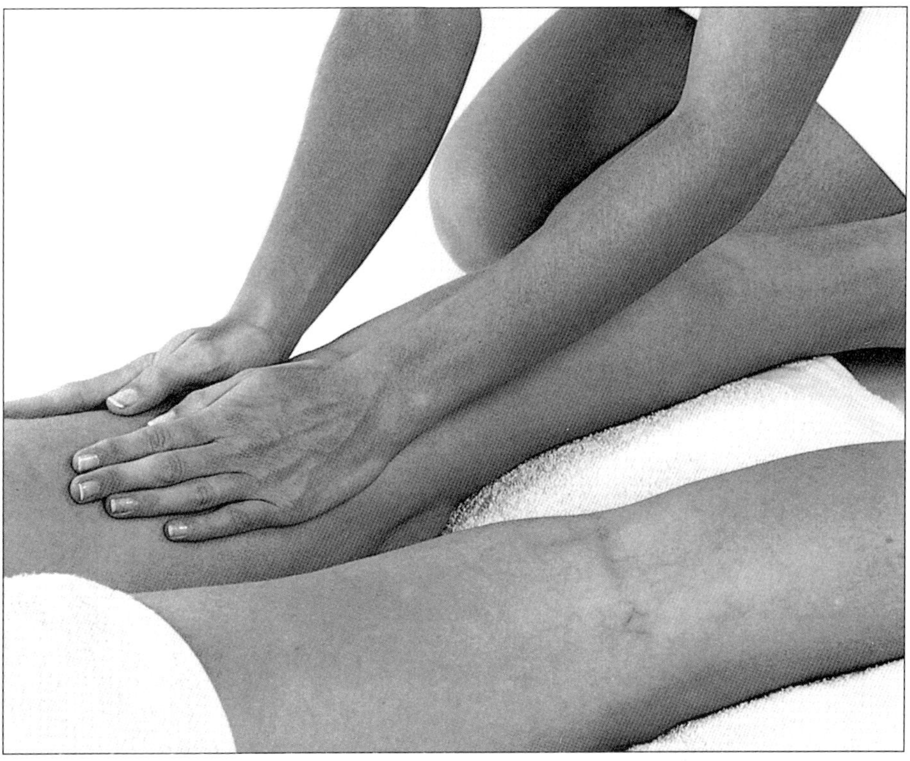

BACK MASSAGE – LOWER BODY

This step-by-step sequence demonstrates the movements on the lower limbs. The photographs follow the natural shape of the legs, consisting of the lower part – from the ankle to the knee – and the top part – from the knee to the hips and buttocks.

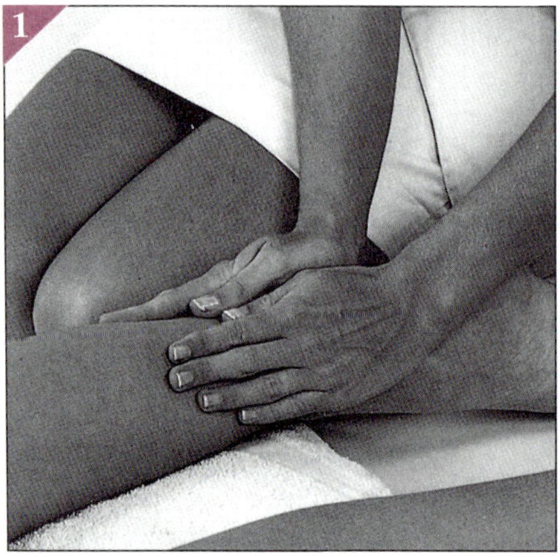

1 Effleurage is performed in an upward direction from the ankle to the buttocks to spread the oil over the whole leg.

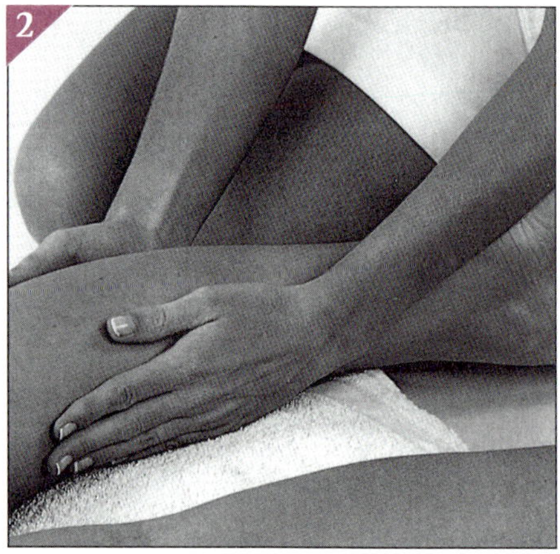

2 The carrier oil should be applied over the surface of the skin; then extend the effleurage to the sides of the leg.

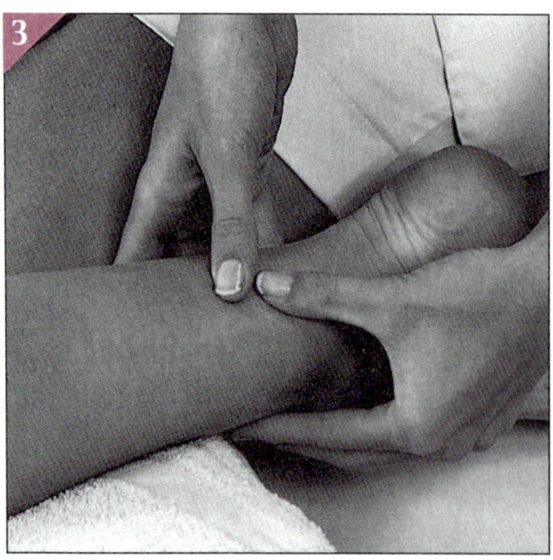

3 Petrissage is performed with both thumbs, working upwards from the ankle to the knee, to 'split' the Gastrocnemius muscle.

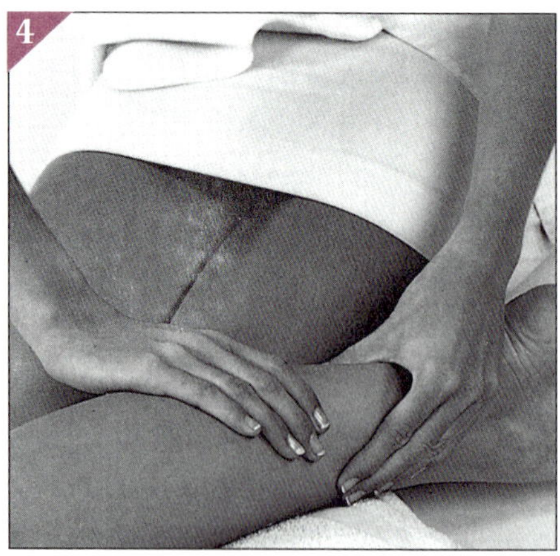

4 Knead the lower part of the leg with both hands, handling the flesh in the direction of the knee.

5 This shows the action of the hands on the lower part of the leg, leading to the massage strokes on the upper part. This movement gives direction and adds fluency to the sequence.

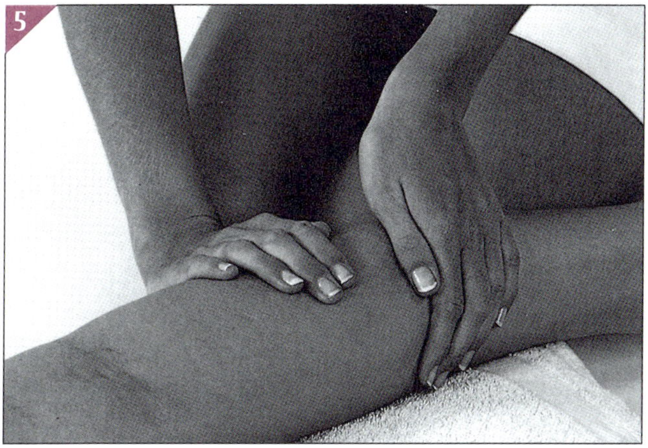

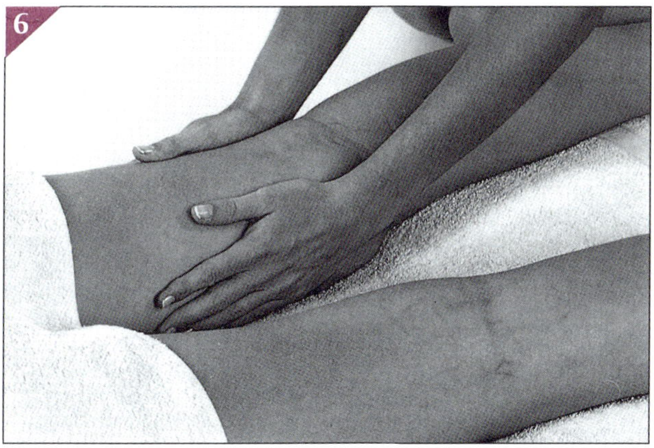

6 Work on the back of the knee joint with the heels of both hands, with the fingers in an upward movement. Then effleurage the upper part of the leg.

7 As shown here, the position of the hands in relation to each other and the upper part of the leg being massaged indicates thorough effleurage movements with pressure and direction.

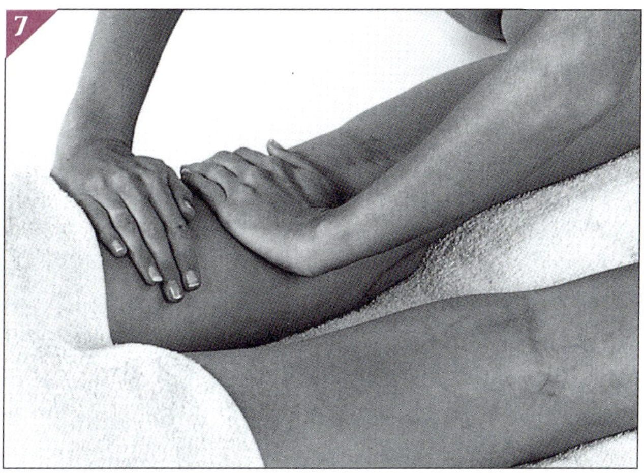

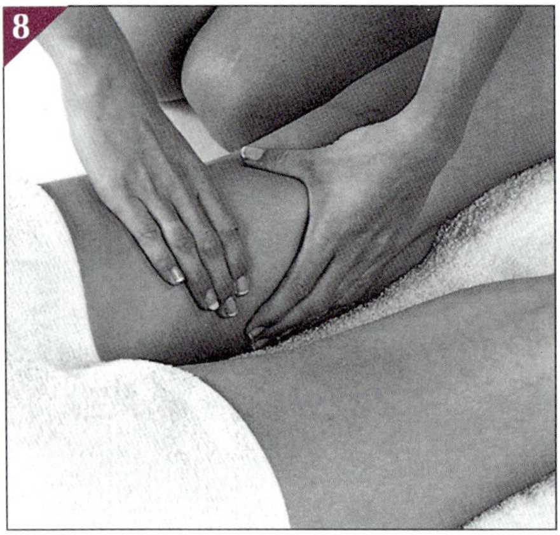

8 It is essential to position the hands correctly when kneading, as shown here on the upper part of the leg.

9 Use a hacking stroke as part of the percussion sequence, as shown, with both hands working on the muscles of the back of the leg.

10 This stroke decongests the muscle and has a toning effect. Apply with firm pressure as an upward movement.

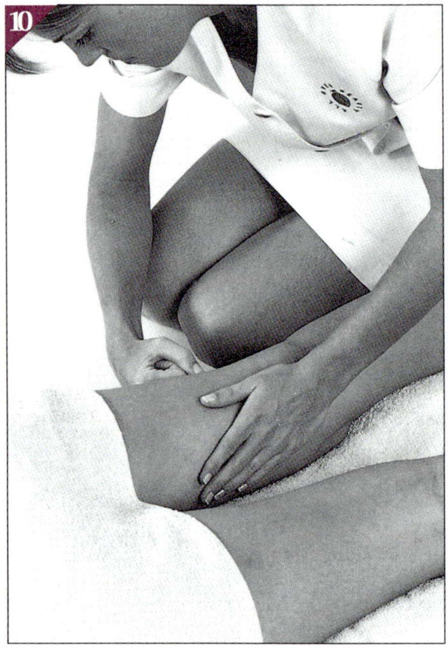

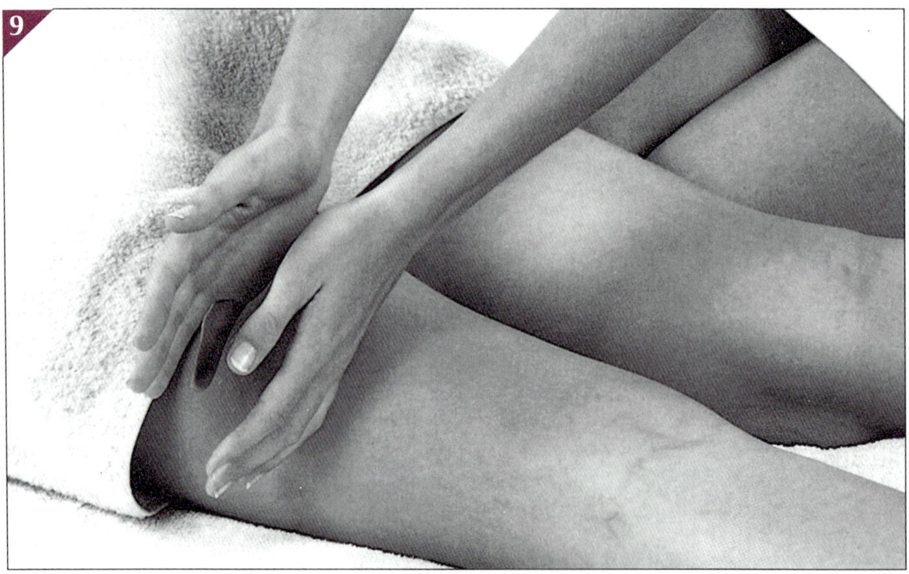

BACK MASSAGE – UPPER BODY

Effleurage of the upper part of the back is best performed with both hands on both sides of the spine. Apply the oil in an upward direction towards the shoulders, gliding gently to meet on the sacrum area. Follow this with deeper, reinforced pressure.

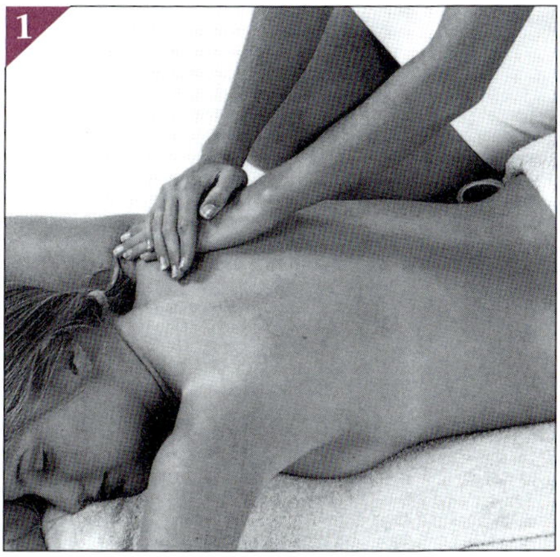

1 Perform reinforced effleurage up the back to the top of the shoulders. This action will give maximum benefit.

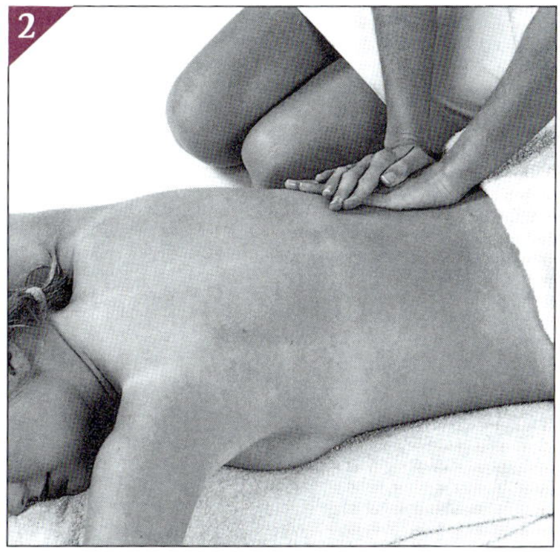

2 Then move back down to the starting position at the base of the spine before moving up to the shoulder blades.

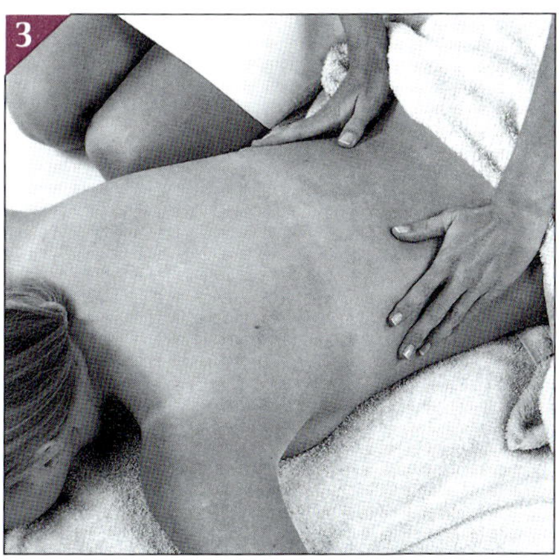

3 Glide the hands slowly down towards the buttocks area with very light pressure to prepare for the friction movement.

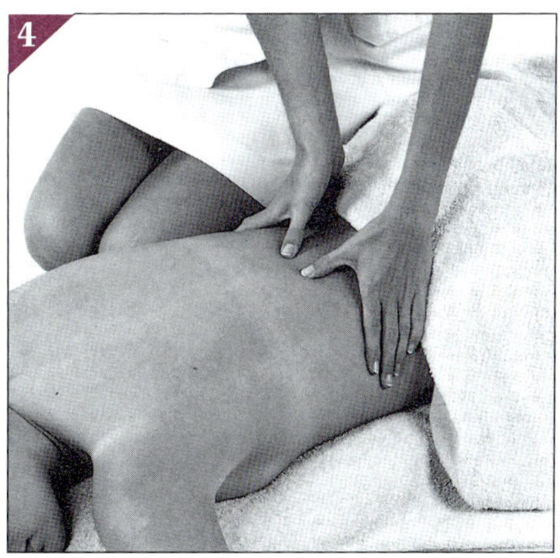

4 Position the thumbs on either side of the spine to perform the petrissage stroke. They should be parallel to the spinal column.

5 With the thumbs pressing down in small circles against the bone underneath, move higher up the spine to start another circling movement. Finish the stroke at the top of the shoulder blades.

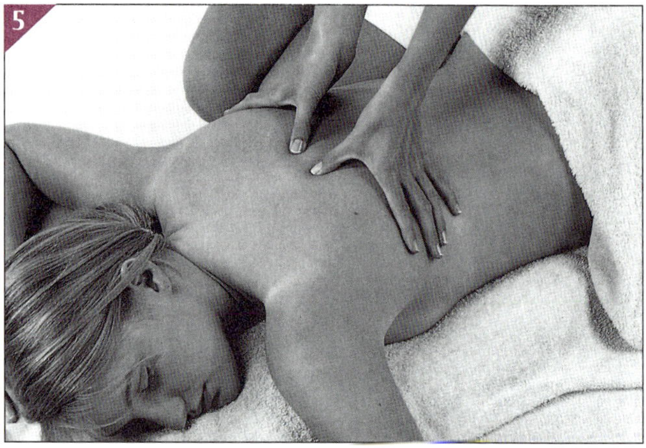

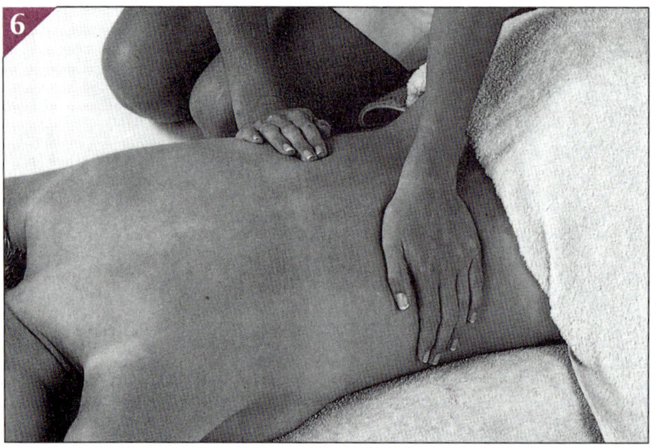

6 The transition to the kneading movement on the back of the body needs to be fluent and the hands must retain contact with the surface of the skin throughout.

7 This shows the correct position of both hands at the start of the kneading sequence, working up from the lower to upper back of the person being massaged.

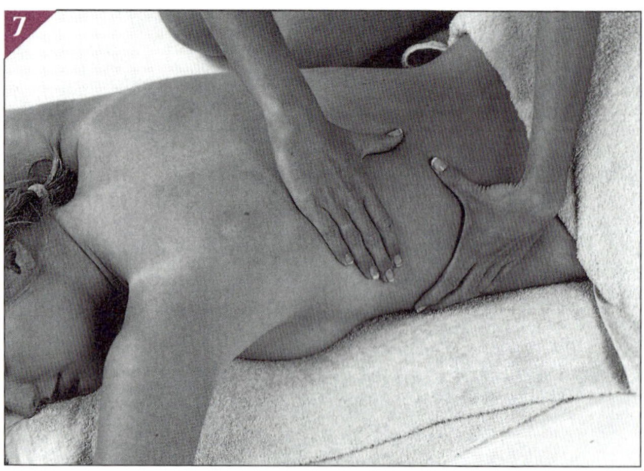

8 This massage stroke is gentle and relaxing although it has a powerful effect. Note the change of the therapist's position in relation to the part of the body being massaged.

9 A reassuring movement of both hands, parting to the sides and over the shoulder blades to add magic to the finishing touch.

10 Both hands are resting gently on both sides of the spine, attuning to the breathing movement of the ribcage.

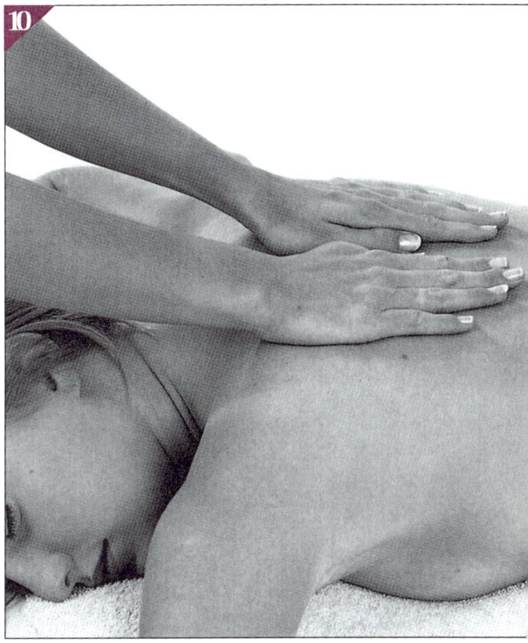

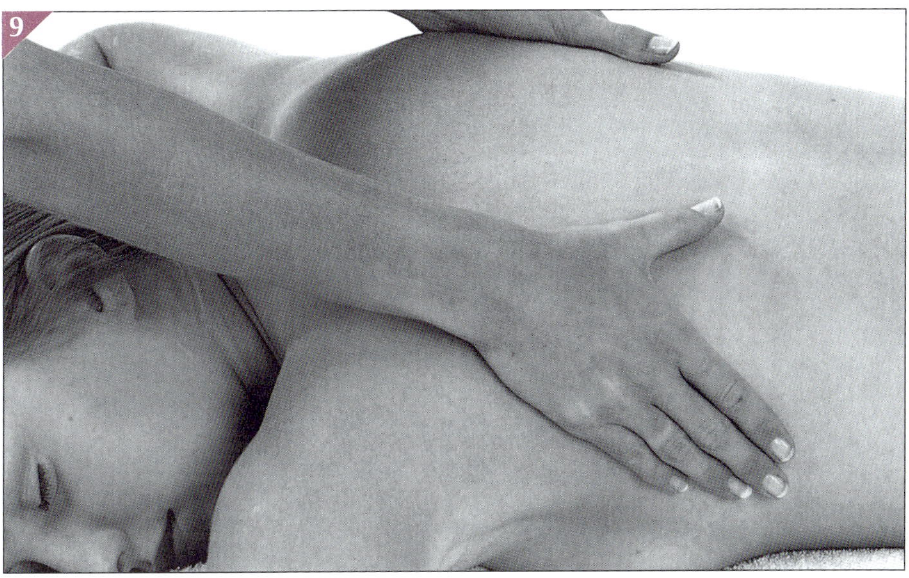

THE FRONT OF THE BODY

Once the back is massaged, turn the person over and treat the front of the body. However, several points need to be remembered so that your massage technique is varied and interesting:

- Arms and legs are elongated body parts, and hence not all massage strokes are applicable. Arms lend themselves to effleurage, petrissage and kneading only.
- To perform the kneading movement, the arm may be lifted off the couch. The lower part of the arm can be stabilized between the crest of the ilium and the therapist's elbow. It is easier to perform kneading with both hands on the top part of the arm.
- The legs may be massaged by using the whole sequence except for the bony lower part from the knee to the ankle. If fleshy enough, all massage movements can be

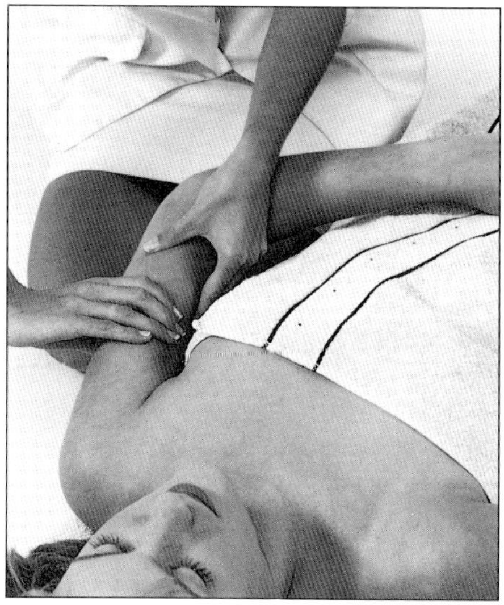

Above and below: effleurage, petrissage and kneading are all effective strokes for massaging the arms and legs. Not all the massage strokes are suitable.

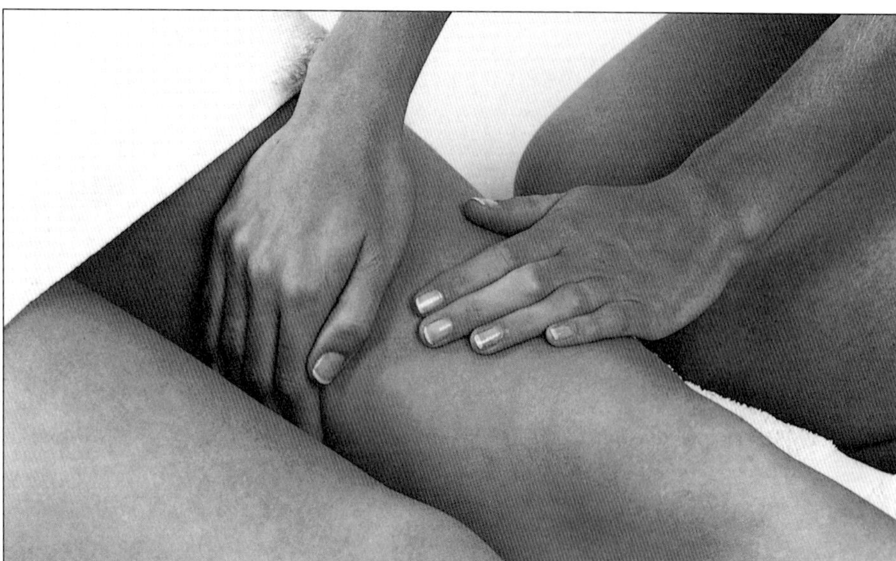

BENEFITS OF MASSAGE

Because 'practice makes perfect' the technique of body massage needs to be applied many times for it to become therapeutic as well as relaxing and pleasurable to the person being massaged. Carry on with the good work and enjoy the treatment every time you perform it. The benefits of massage, performed on a regular basis, are manifold.

- Massage has an impact on all body systems.
- It relaxes and stimulates.
- It tones up and rids the body of muscular and nervous tension.
- It is an effective therapy in relieving stress, promoting health and happiness.
- The body's energy level is restored by massage as well as the proper functioning of the previously stiff joints and muscles.
- Massage eases stiffness and discomfort, helping the body to excrete the toxins.
- It is one of the most natural ways to help people deal with the physical, mental and emotional stresses of modern living.
- The increased sense of emotional well-being rejuvenates emotional resources in the recipient's body.
- Memory and the decision-making process can both be improved by body massage.
- Massage can bring emotional stability, which can help to increase confidence and relaxation. These assets are necessary in a one-to-one relationship not only at home but also in the workplace.

applied on the top part of the leg resting on the treatment couch.

- The area of the abdomen is very sensitive because it houses the solar plexus. A kneading stroke may be applied with the flat surface between the knuckles of the therapist's hand forming a fist. Pressure should be adjusted to match the sensitivity of the abdomen being massaged. All movements should be performed in a circular fashion, clockwise from the point of the appendix on the right-hand side following the colon (ascending, transverse and descending) to the left side of the abdominal cavity.
- The therapist's hand has to be in contact at all times with the skin surface of the abdomen and the change from one stroke to another should not be permitted to interrupt the fluency of the sequence.

Right: light effleurage movements can be used in abdominal massage.

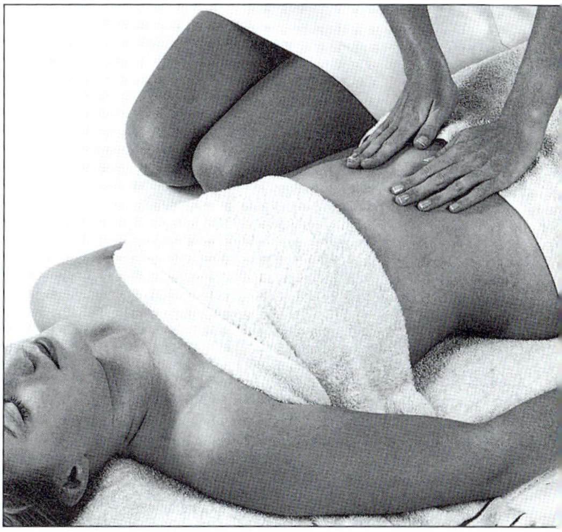

FRONT MASSAGE – LOWER BODY

When you have completed the upper body massage, it is time to move on to the lower body. Make sure that you cover the upper body with some towels to keep it warm while you work on the legs of the person being massaged. Continue as shown below.

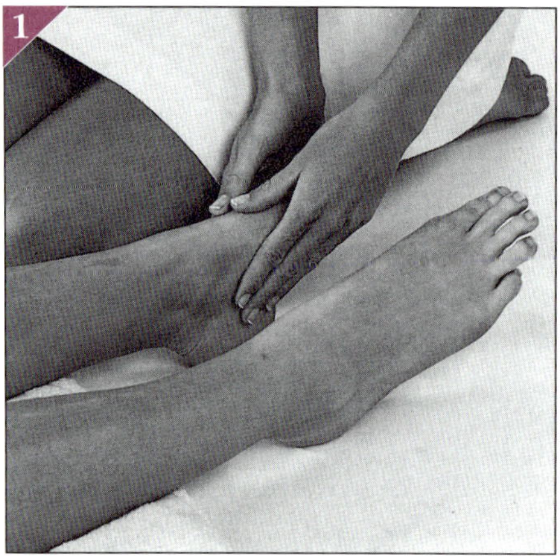

1 Start with effleurage of the top of the foot, gently but firmly stroking, with the hands ready to treat the ankle area.

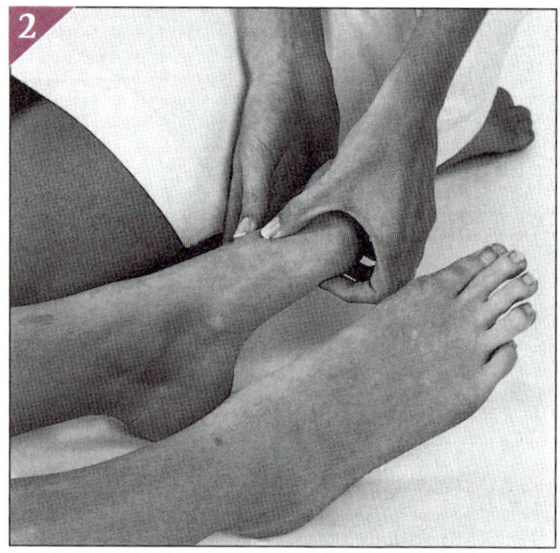

2 Now move on to petrissage movements on the top of the foot. This photo shows the correct positioning of the hands.

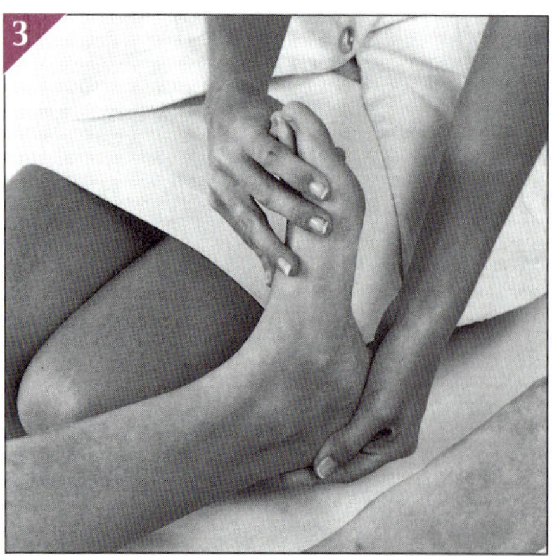

3 Stretching and joint mobilization is performed. If wished, this can be done earlier in preparation for foot and leg massage.

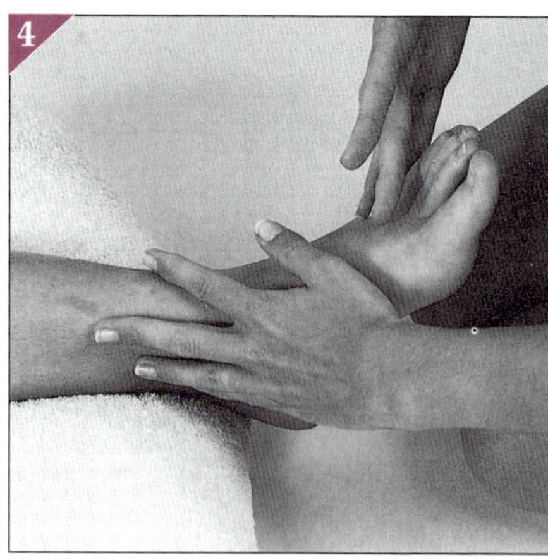

4 Gentle feathering strokes are used to relax the foot being treated in between the other massage movements.

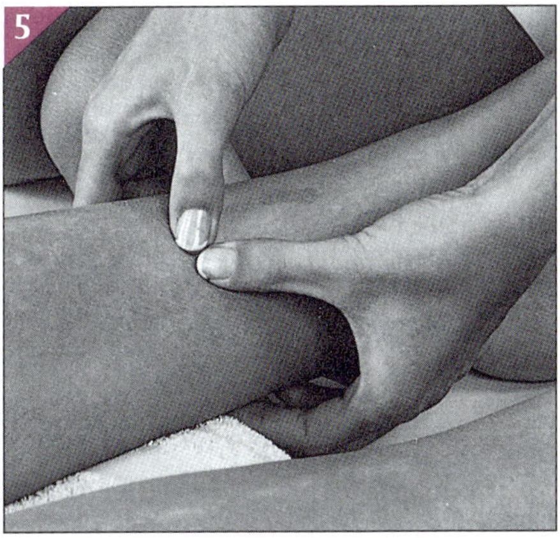

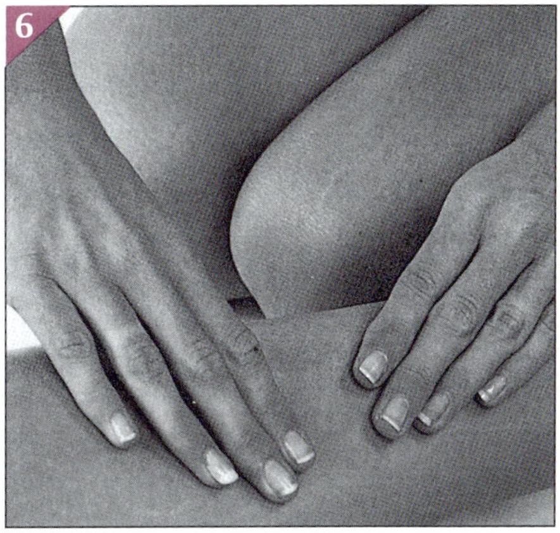

5 Move slowly up from the foot to treat the ankle area and the lower leg, pressing in gently with your thumbs.

6 Now perform the kneading stroke on the front of the leg, using the correct hand positions and pressing down lightly.

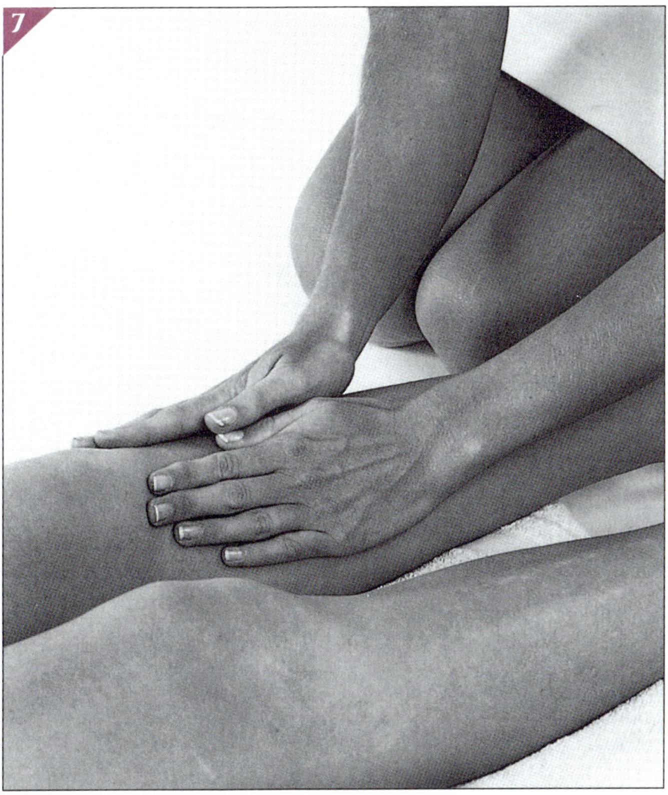

7 Finish the massage of the lower leg with some relaxing effleurage strokes. Repeat on the other foot and lower leg before moving on to the upper legs.

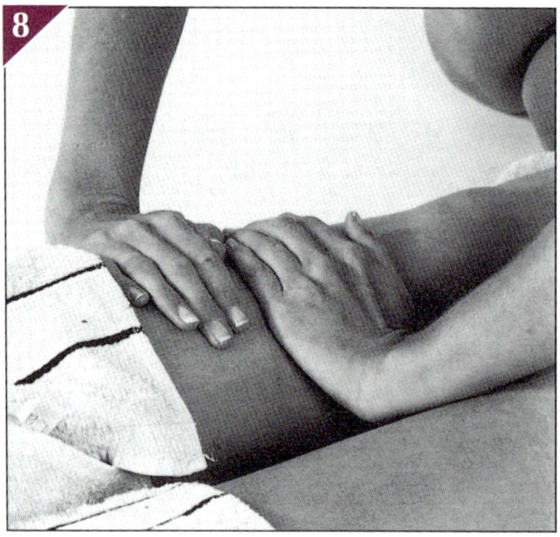

8 This shows the position of the hands for effleurage movements performed on the top of the front of the leg.

9 Now move on to petrissage movements, placing the heels of your hands on either side of the knee.

10 Finish the leg massage with some more gentle effleurage strokes. This shows the return stroke on the upper leg.

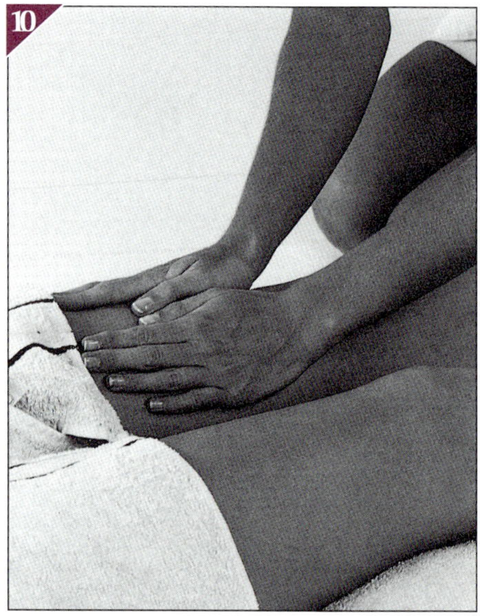

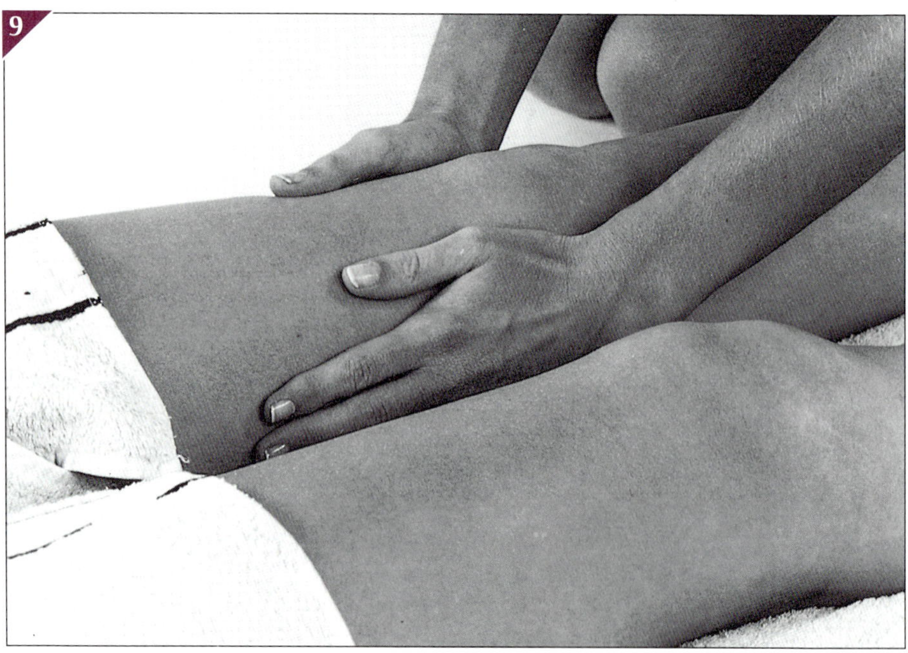

FRONT MASSAGE – UPPER BODY

1 Start the upper body (front) massage with effleurage strokes on both sides of the abdomen.

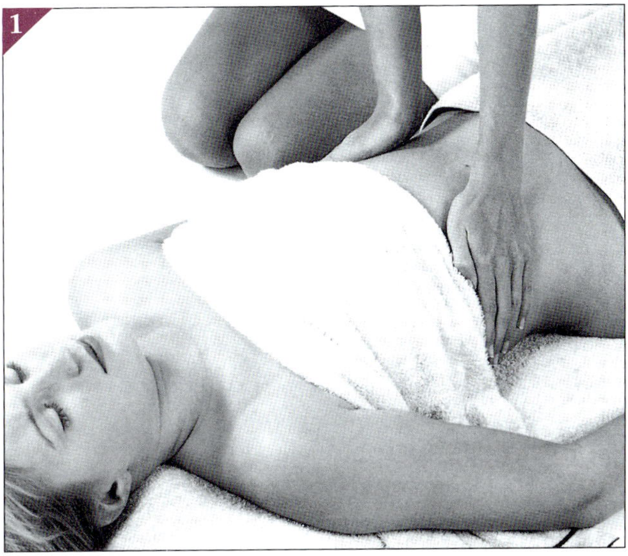

2 Now gently knead the sides of the abdomen, lifting up and squeezing the flesh between the fingers and thumb, then releasing it.

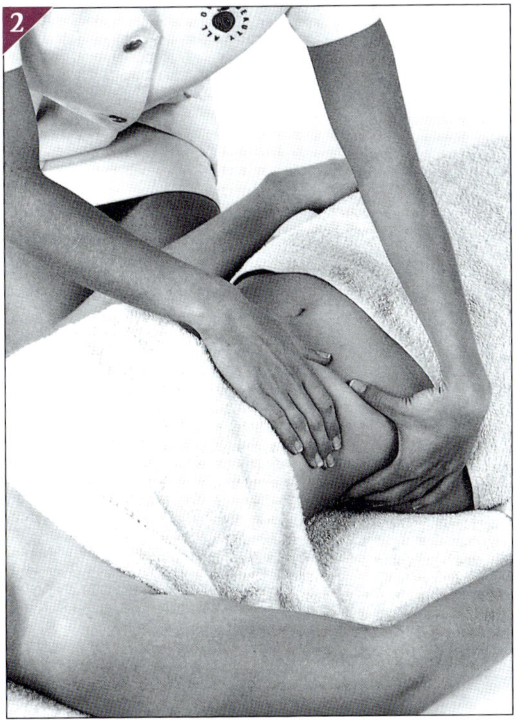

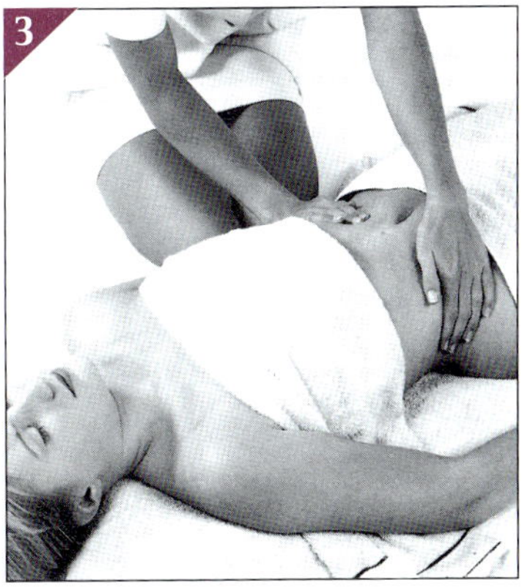

3 Use a gentle sideways stroke to aid lymph drainage and relaxation in the recipient of the massage. The abdomen is a very sensitive area and any massage strokes used should be light and gentle.

4 Finish off with some kneading, using both hands on the abdominal area.

4

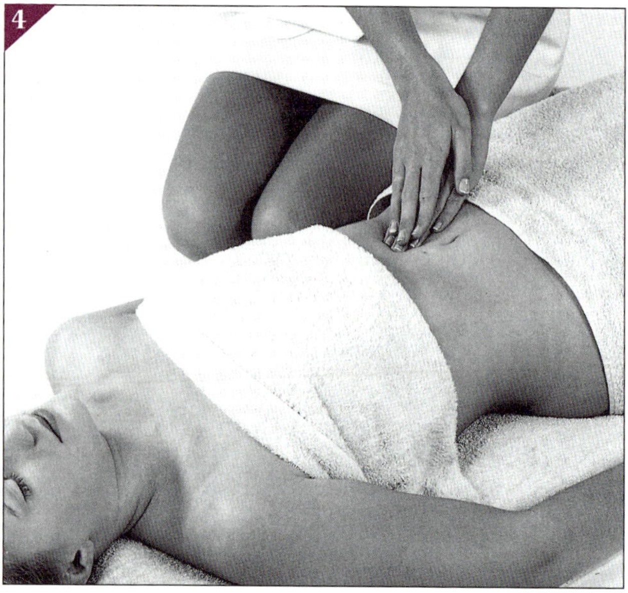

5 This is the way to handle the arms when performing effleurage on the lower part of the arm.

5

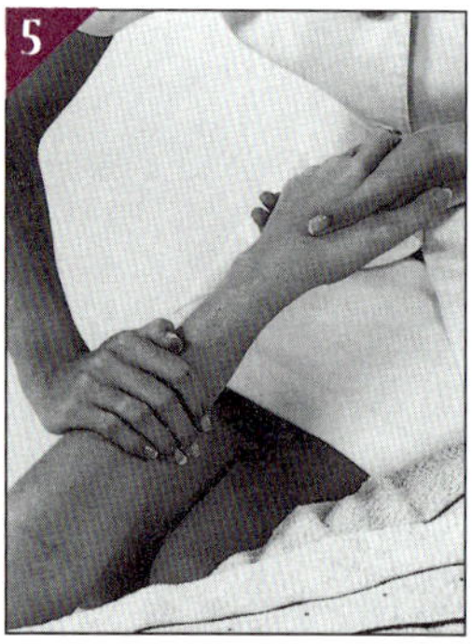

6

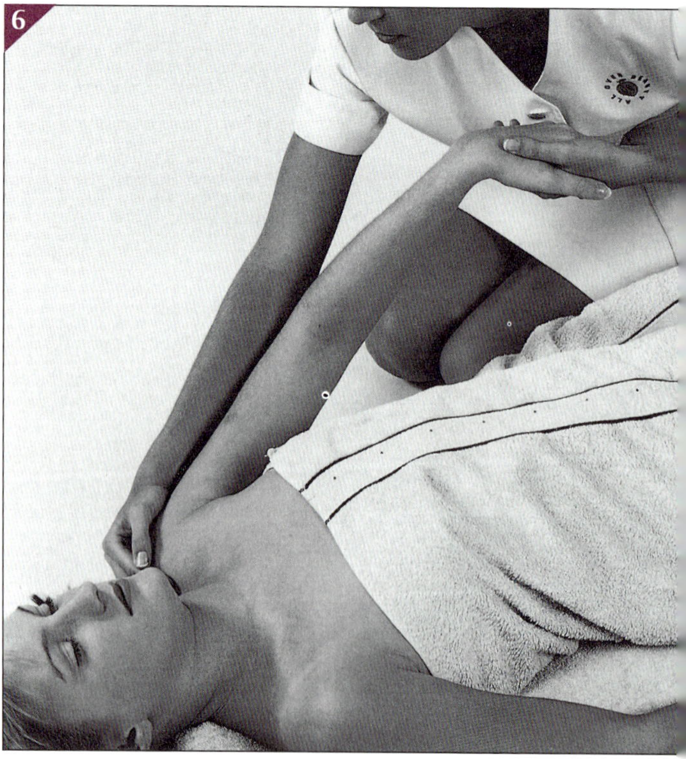

6 This demonstrates the full movement of effleurage over the shoulder joint with the therapist in a comfortable handling position.

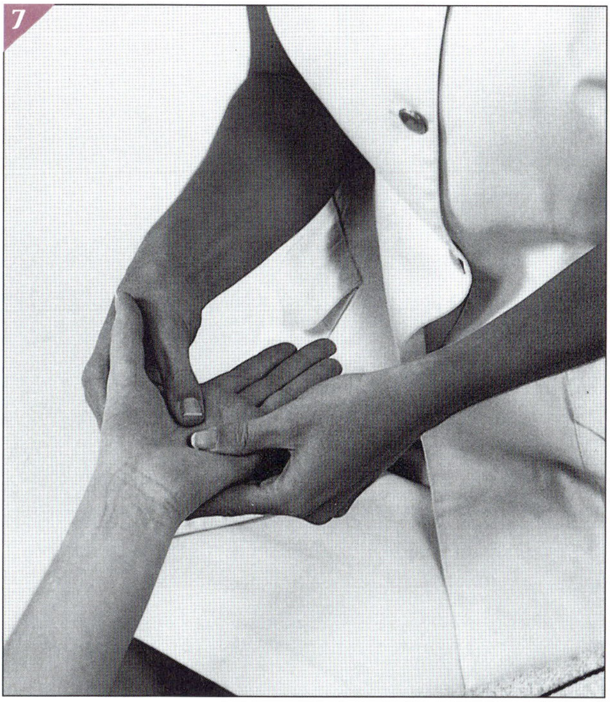

7 Friction is used on the palm of the hand to disperse congestion and to relax the hand.

8 This shows mobilization of the wrist joint as part of the arm massage.

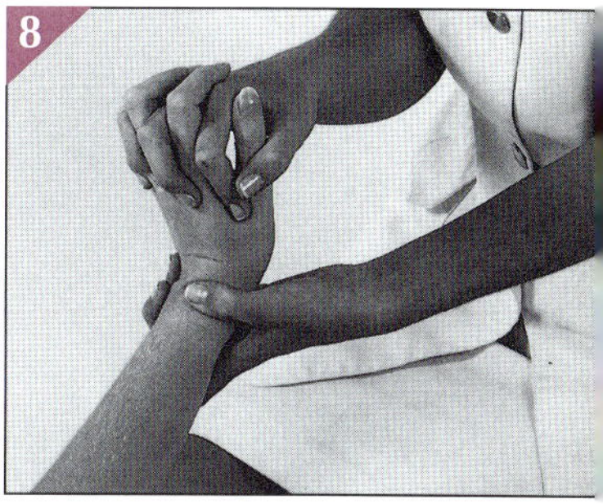

9 Knead the lower arm below the elbow, with the arm resting on a couch to reduce tension. Repeat the sequence on the other arm.

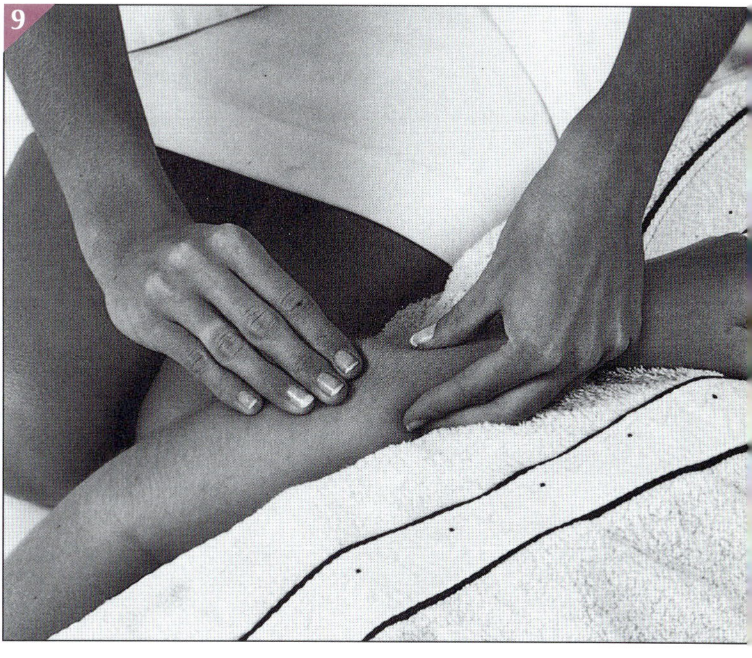

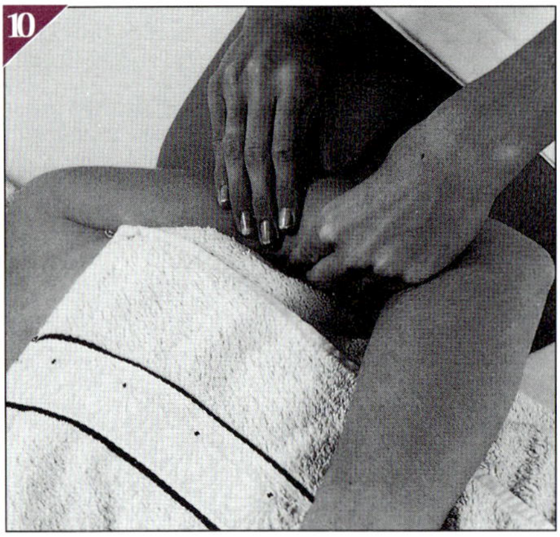

10 Now work your way up the upper arm to the shoulder, gently kneading and squeezing the flesh as you go. Repeat on the other arm.

11 Friction movement is performed across the upper chest and shoulder blades to aid lymph drainage of the shoulders, in a supine position.

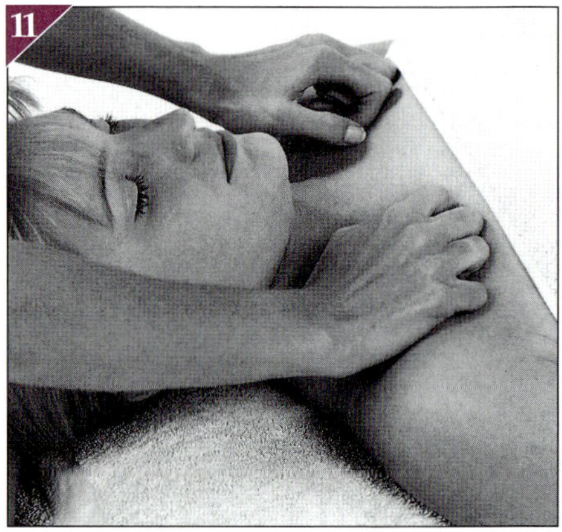

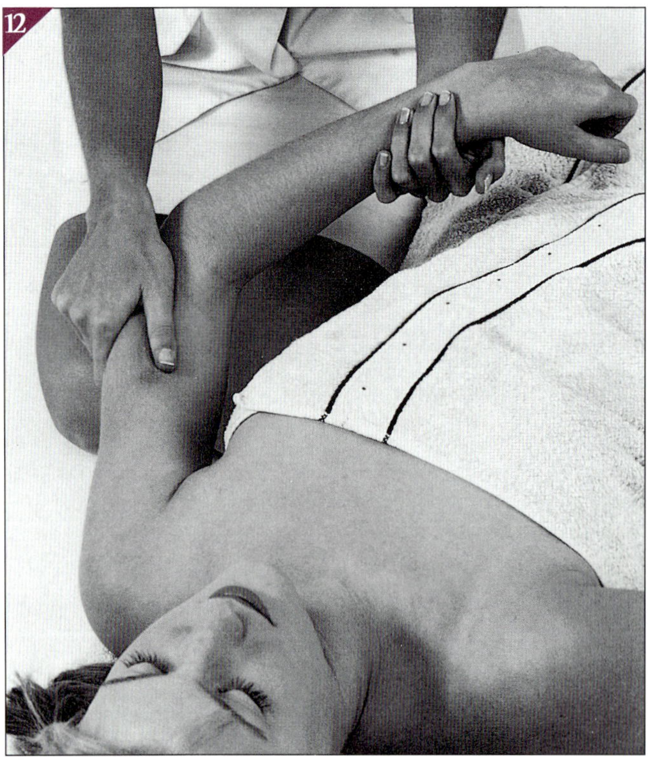

12 The upper body massage finishes with friction strokes being performed on the upper part of the arm, and then some gentle, relaxing effleurage.

FRONT MASSAGE – HEAD AND NECK

1 Before starting the neck and head massage, go behind the person being massaged and gently stretch the neck.

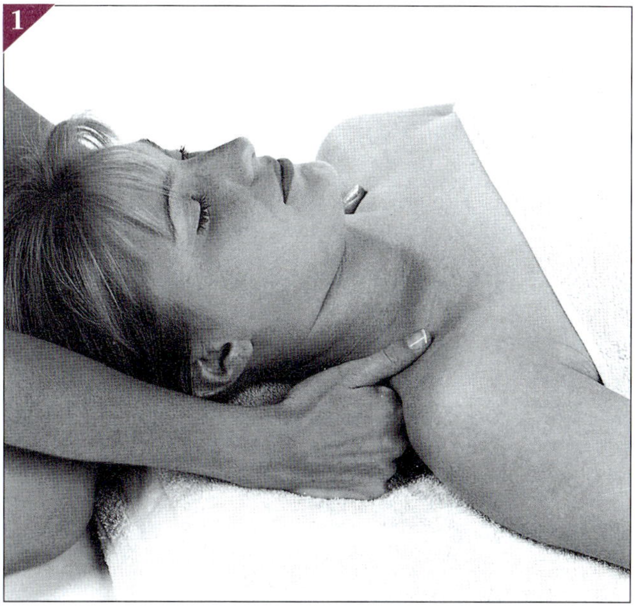

2 With the person in a supine position, perform upward effleurage of the neck, taking care to be gentle but firm.

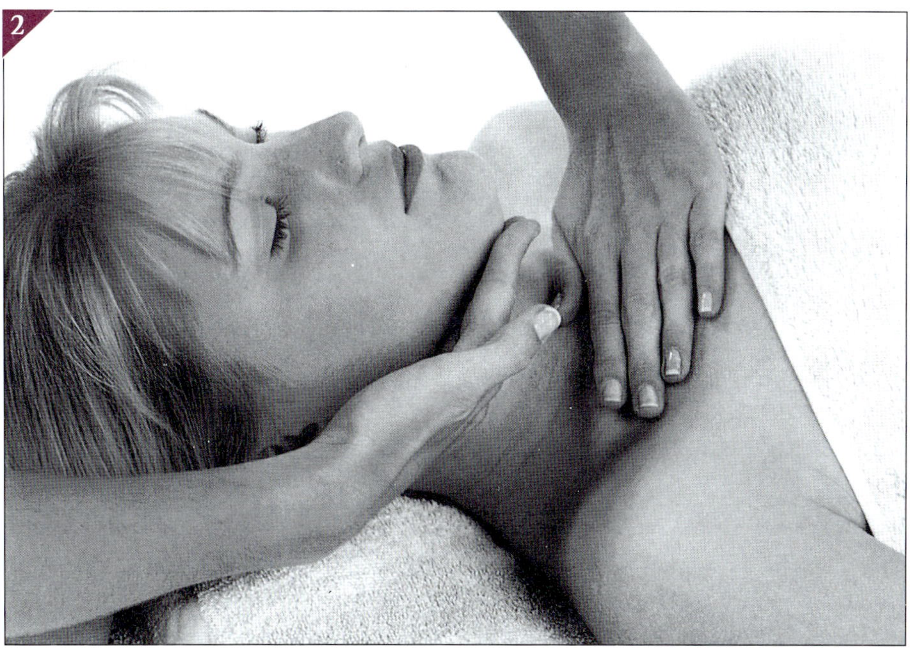

3 Move up the neck to the chin area and perform some tapotement (gentle striking movements) on the neck and chin.

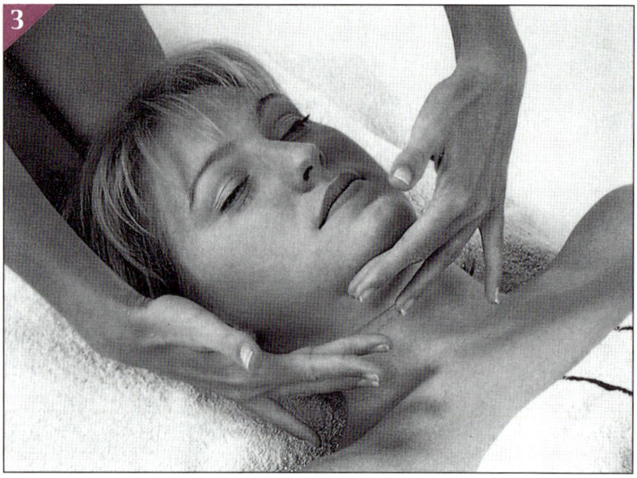

4 A balancing movement is used in face massage to help energy distribution for relaxation.

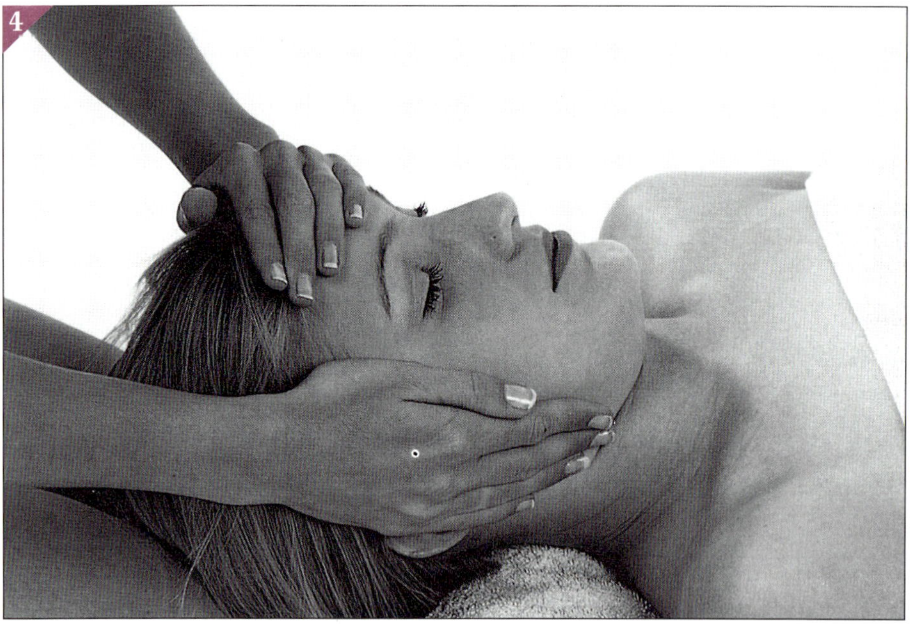

5 Sideways effleurage of the forehead is the next part of the face massage. Make sure that the head of the person being massaged is well supported throughout the massage session. Use pillows or a rolled-up towel.

6 The face and neck massage comes to an end with friction and stretching the neck out gently to stimulate drainage. The full body massage is now complete and the person being massaged should feel relaxed and refreshed.

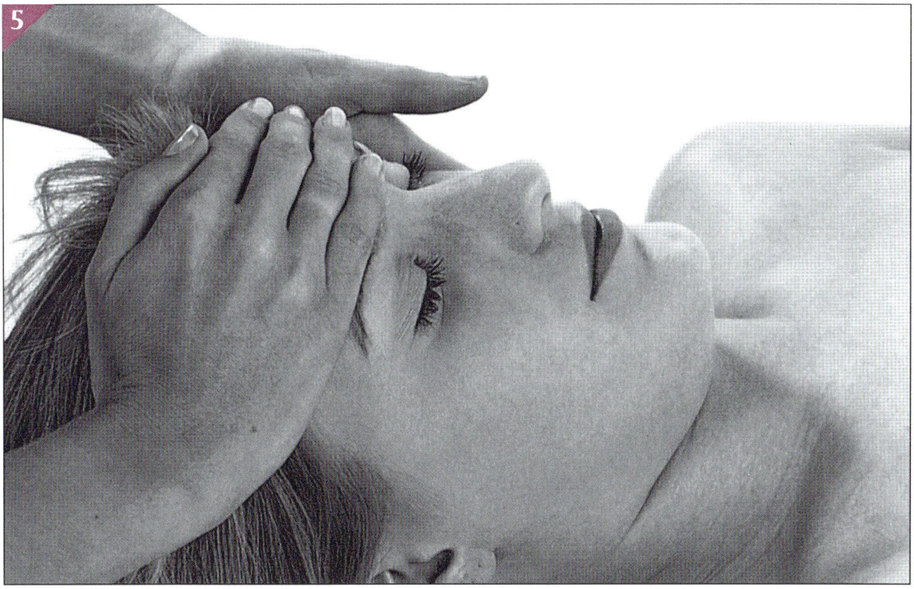
5

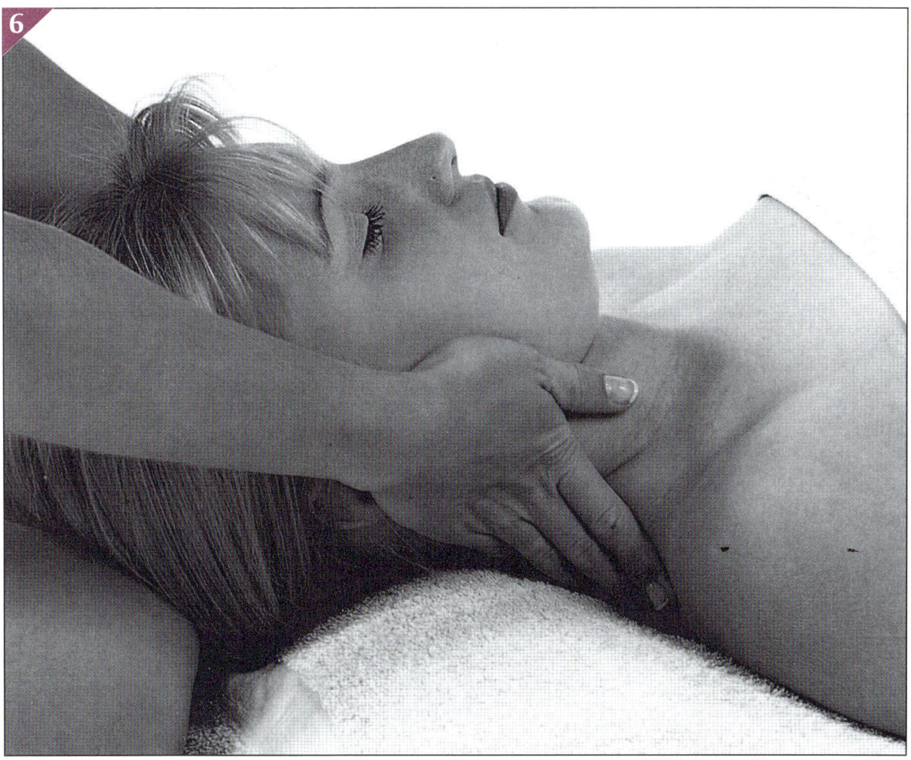
6

CHAPTER FOUR

4

AROMATHERAPY MASSAGE

Aromatherapy is a treatment modality which uses essential oils obtained from plants – flowers, trees and herbs – to heal a wide range of illnesses and conditions. The relevant plant is put through a process of extraction whereby a volatile substance is extracted and this liquid is called an essential oil. There are several methods of extraction such as distillation – the most popular method – maceration, pressing and dissolving in volatile solvents. Aromatherapy massage is applied by using essential oils extracted from plants as an aid to massage.

Below: aromatherapy massage is both relaxing and therapeutic. It can be used to treat a wide range of health problems.

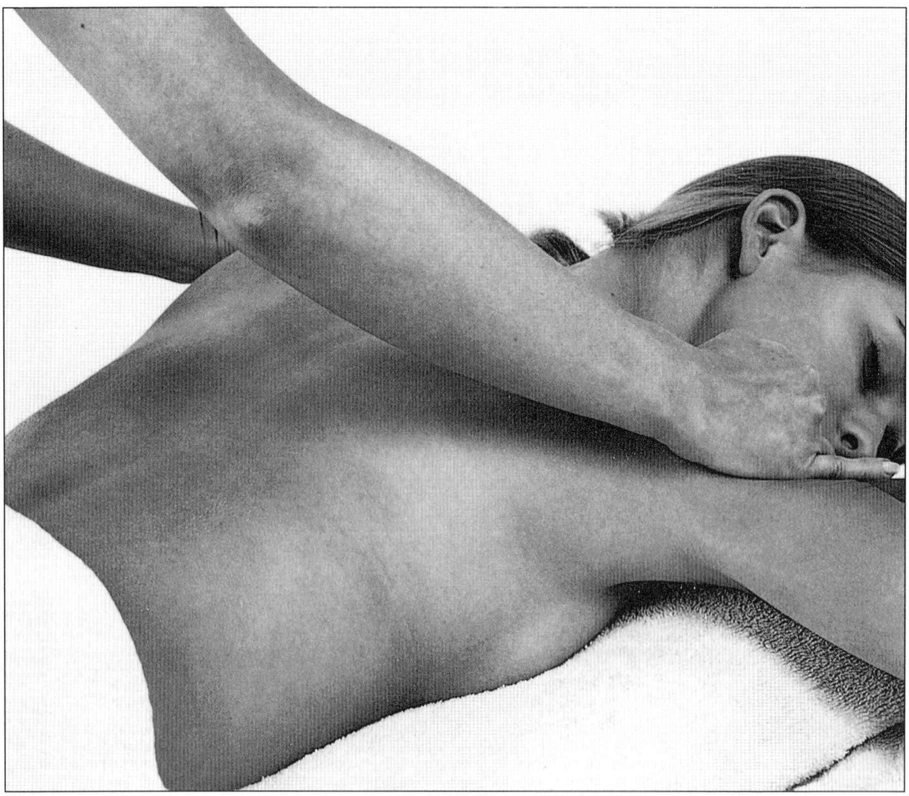

Origins and Uses of Essential Oils

Aromatic plants and infused oils were used extensively throughout the history of civilization. In ancient Rome, Greece and Egypt, people used these preparations as an aid to beauty and for health reasons. The infused material was blended into a body massage oil or used in a carrier, such as an ointment or cream, for external application.

Essential oils were used not only in massage therapy but also in the bath, for inhalation, or even ingestion. However, internal application of essential oils can be practised only under the supervision of an experienced aromatherapist.

Characteristics of Essential Oils

Essential oils are odorous and volatile and some readily evaporate in the open air. Their consistency is more like water than oil. They have a complex chemical structure, but generally contain alcohols, esters, ketones, aldehydes and terpenes. The aromatic materials are formed in the chloroplasts of the leaf where they combine with glucose to form glucosides which are conveyed round the plant structures.

The pure essential oils, with the exception of the citrus oils, are generally long lasting and, provided that they are stored in dark glass bottles with stoppers away from direct sunlight, can last for a long time (some mature with age) without losing their therapeutic powers. They have the properties of the plant from which they have been extracted but have the advantage of being much more convenient to use. Pure essential oils are concentrated plant extracts and hence they are used only in drops and are stored in small glass bottles with droppers.

The sense of smell is connected to our emotions and it therefore plays the largest part in recognising the power of aromatherapy. We can experience how

A Word of Warning

When using essential oils, remember that they are very powerful – in Europe they are regarded as a form of medicine. They are dispensed by doctors and pharmacists and used only by experienced, professionally qualified practitioners.

The advent of extended research in recent decades demonstrates clearly that essential oils have to be treated with due respect and care. Some oils are very safe and these may be called good 'all-rounders'. In this classification are included Lavender oil, Chamomile and Eucalyptus. However, citrus fruit oils can be skin sensitizers since they increase its photosensitivity and consequently they have to be used carefully in the summer. Do not expose your skin to the sun immediately after using them.

Origins of Aromatherapy

The origins are lost in the mists of time when healers of antiquity practised their primitive forms of natural medicine. The Egyptian embalmers sought aromatic herbs, woods and resins to mummify cats, monkeys, important dignitaries and Pharaohs, achieving the ultimate goal of arresting the putrefaction of corpses by harnessing the antiseptic power of natural essences.

One of the founders of Pharaohic medicine was the architect Imhotep. However, it was under the heretic sun-king Akhenaton that the use of pure essential oils in the art of medicine was brought to its full glory. The city of Akhenaton was built according to the best rules of hygiene – in its public squares piles of aromatic substances were burnt to purify the air.

In ancient Greece, the knowledge of pure essential oils was taught in the school of Cos, graced by Hippocrates whom the Greeks named the Father of Medicine. The Romans, including Celsius and Galen, also supported the use of natural plant oils for some medical purposes.

The Arabs were instrumental in spreading the remedies from Asia Minor and the Middle East to Europe and to the shores of the Mediterranean. They improved the methods of extracting essential oils, perfected the apparatus for distillation and made up new elixirs and ointments. Later, the great European navigators of the fifteenth century brought back new plants and aromas from their distant voyages.

However, after the Renaissance the popularity of aromatherapy waned as some pharmacists developed new chemical syntheses and offered compounds which were held to be capable of replacing natural oils.

We have to acknowledge that the skill of embalming organisms by the diffusion of aromatic preparations through the skin is an amazing art and our Pharmacopoeia was obliged to preserve a great deal of their aroma-based medicines until the beginning of the twentieth century.

certain pure essential oils have the power to lift depression or have a calming influence on the troubled emotional side of our life when we are under stress.

Most of the essences are clear, although some are coloured: blue (Chamomile), green (Rose) or brown (Cinnamon). The essences are soluble in alcohol and carrier oils (preferably of vegetable origin). Essential oils are present in droplets in a large number of plants, particularly those used for culinary or medical purposes. They can occur in the roots (Calamus), leaves (Rosemary), flowers (Chamomile), wood (Cedarwood and Sandalwood), resins (Myrrh) and the peel of some fruits, such as lemons, oranges and grapefruits.

Harvesting

The essences are usually extracted by distillation, which is one of the most popular methods of extraction of essential oils. However, the raw material must be picked at a specific time of the year for oil extraction. Even the prevailing weather conditions and the time of day during harvesting are important for determining the quality of the essential oil that is extracted. This is because whilst they are in the plant the essences are constantly changing their composition and move from one part of the plant to another, according to the season and the time of day.

The aroma and chemical constituents of the essences change with different soil conditions, methods of cultivation and changes in climate. This is why essential oils from certain countries, such as Sandalwood from Mysore and Jasmine from Morocco, are considered to be of higher quality than those from other countries.

Top, Middle and Base Notes

The high rate of evaporation of essential oils is an important factor to consider when blending a well-balanced product. The volatility rate varies in different oils and all pure essential oils can be divided into three categories: Top Notes, Middle Notes and Base Notes.

- **Top Note** essential oils are the fastest acting but the quickest to evaporate. They are also the most stimulating and uplifting to mind and body.
- Pure essential oils in the **Middle Note** group are moderately volatile. They primarily affect the functions of the body, e.g. respiratory system, digestive system, and the general metabolism of the body.
- The **Base Note** essential oils are slower to evaporate. They are the most sedating and relaxing. They are often blended with Top Note oils, which helps to sustain the volatility of the particular pure essential oil of this classification.

Choose Quality Oils

The price of an essential oil can be correlated to the results obtained and it is worthwhile to use the best quality oils for aromatherapy in order to achieve the best results. Whilst all essential oils appear to be relatively expensive, some like Rose or Jasmine require large amounts of raw material to produce a small amount of essential oil, whereas Eucalyptus may yield a much greater quantity of essential oil. This is why essential oils can differ so much in price.

Preparing Massage Oils

Pure essential oils can be blended in many carrier oils for aromatherapy treatment. They can also be blended in a cream or a balm base. Essential oils are very versatile indeed and can be used in inhalation, vapourization, body massage, compresses and as gargles or mouthwashes.

Carrier Oils

For body massage oil, the carrier oil has to be of vegetable origin – oils of mineral origin are not suitable. The vegetable oil will enhance energy flow during and after treatment and will nourish the skin without causing allergic reaction. However, mineral oil will make it impossible for pure essential oils to penetrate the skin and will impair energy flow.

There is a great variety of carrier oils to choose from depending upon the skin type, nature of the complaint being treated, the recipient's age and preference. The most commonly used carrier oils include:

- Sweet almond oil
- Apricot kernel oil
- Grapeseed oil
- Sesame seed oil
- Peach kernel oil

In order to choose wisely, you should refer back to page 17.

CAUTION

You should always remember when applying essential oils that they permeate through the skin and end up in the bloodstream, performing healing from the inside. The point of entry may also be via the lungs but the effect is exactly the same, with the oils working from within the recipient's body.

BLENDING THE OIL

To an eggcupful of carrier oil, you should add two or three drops of essential oil. Stir the blend with your finger and then check the aroma.

- The blend for a relaxing aromatherapy treatment may contain essential oils of Lavender, Chamomile, Rose, Neroli or Jasmine.
- For coughs and colds, the blend may introduce Eucalyptus oil, Niaouli, Pine or Cajuput.
- Stretch marks may be treated with Lavender, Myrrh and Patchouli.
- Insomnia can be counteracted by the use of Marjoram, Rose, Neroli, Clary Sage or Chamomile essential oils.

CHECKLIST

- Check that the prepared blend is to hand and the environment is warm and relaxing with a supply of warm towels.
- Ask the person receiving aromatherapy treatment to visit the toilet prior to treatment, as aromatherapy stimulates the bodily systems.
- Make sure that you are relaxed and at ease before commencing treatment as any tension on your part will be transmitted to the receiving person and you will not achieve your objective of a happy, relaxed patient.
- Your fingernails should be short so as not to scratch the skin surface, and your hands should be warm.
- Put on relaxing music and then start learning the absorbing techniques of aromatherapy massage.

THE MASSAGE

The aim of aromatherapy treatment is to encourage thorough penetration of the essential oil used and to create a state of relaxation in the person being massaged. The massage will stimulate the blood and lymph circulation and also speed up the elimination of toxins from the system. The essential oils will act as a form of preventative medicine by encouraging the proper functioning of all bodily systems, particularly the nervous system.

THE BACK

1 Place about one teaspoonful of massage oil in the palm of one hand and rub both hands together.

1

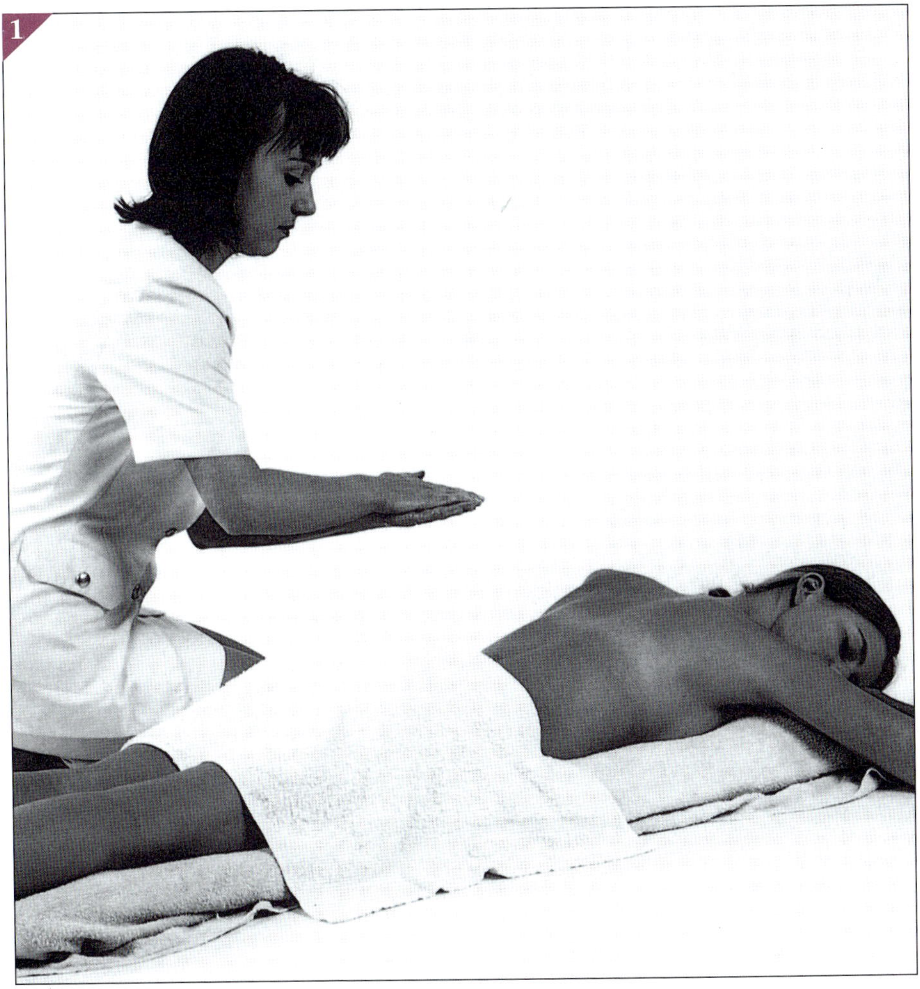

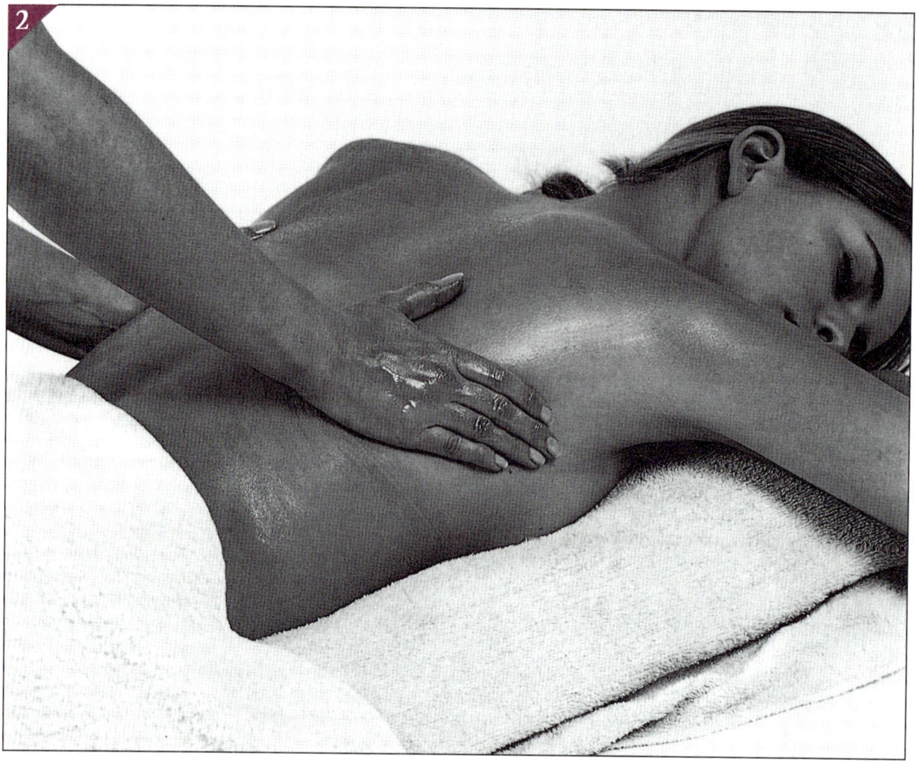

2 Spread the oil over the whole back with effleurage movements. With fingers facing the shoulders, position the hands at the base of the spine and stroke firmly in an upward movement on each side of the spine. Go round the shoulder blade and very lightly, in a sliding movement, down the back to the base of the spine. Use the whole hand. This movement can be repeated several times.

3 With one hand over the other, go up between the shoulder blades, and round the right shoulder. Cross the spine upwards and move up across to the other shoulder blade. Repeat this movement several times.

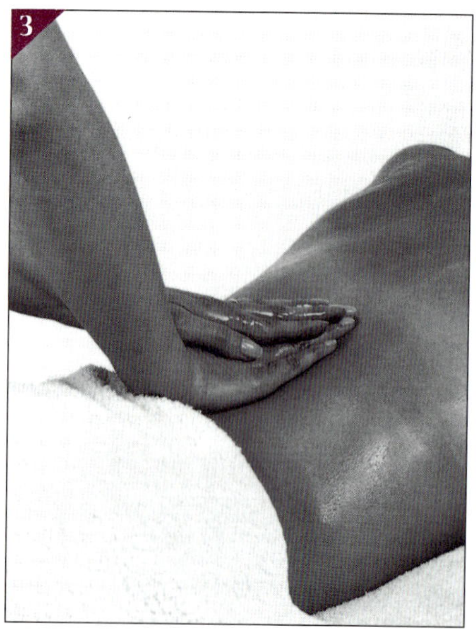

4 Bring your hands back to the base of the spine on the last repeat but make sure that you are holding the whole of your reinforced hand on the body.

5 Place both thumbs together and facing each other in the spinal channel of the neck at the left side of the spine.

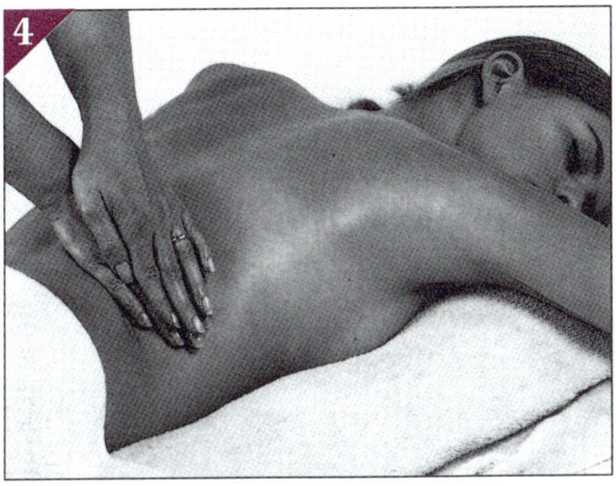

4

6 Pressing firmly down with your thumbs and releasing, move 2.5cm (1in) further down and repeat these

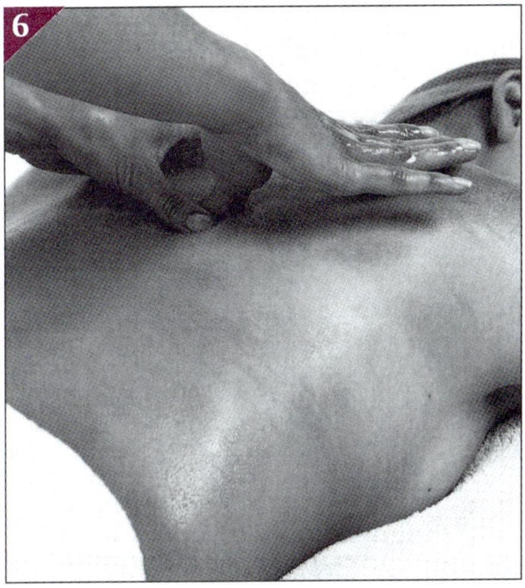

6

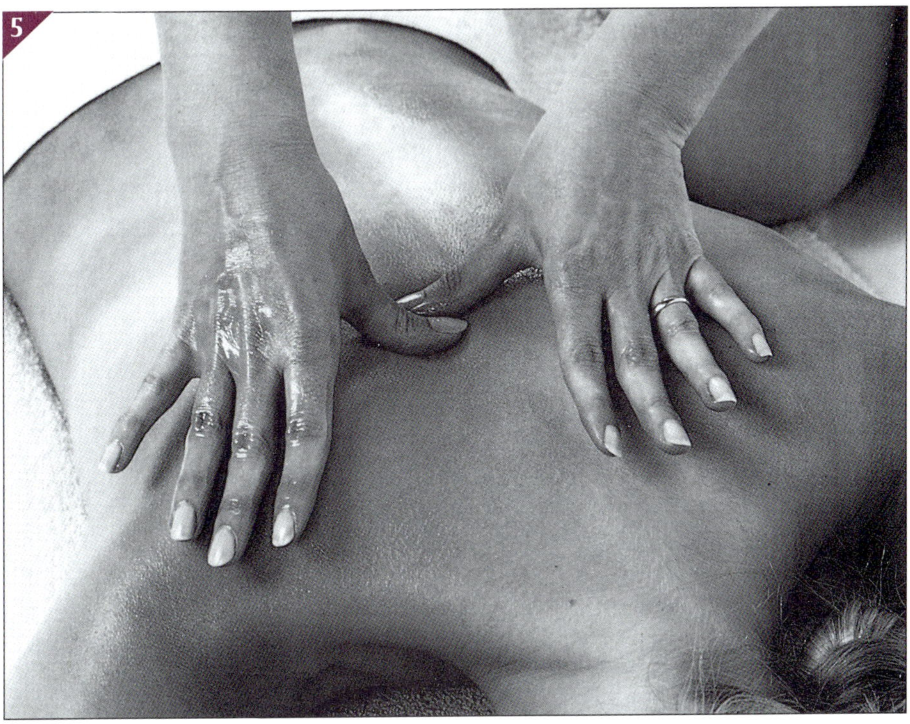

5

movements to sacrum level. Slide gently to the right of the top of the spinal channel and, keeping the thumbs together, work in a downward movement to right hip level, in rhythmical pace attuning to the breathing action of the person being massaged.

Introduce gentle effleurage, sliding back without pressure, on both sides of the body. Move up and out towards the armpits, returning the same way without pressure. Each time you move out, start lower down the spine until the last return will reach the last rib of the ribcage. Repeat the movement several times. Introduce effleurage again, and repeat the stroke as required.

7 With alternate hands at hip level on the left side of the recipient's back, push down with the fingers facing the shoulders at the side of the spine.

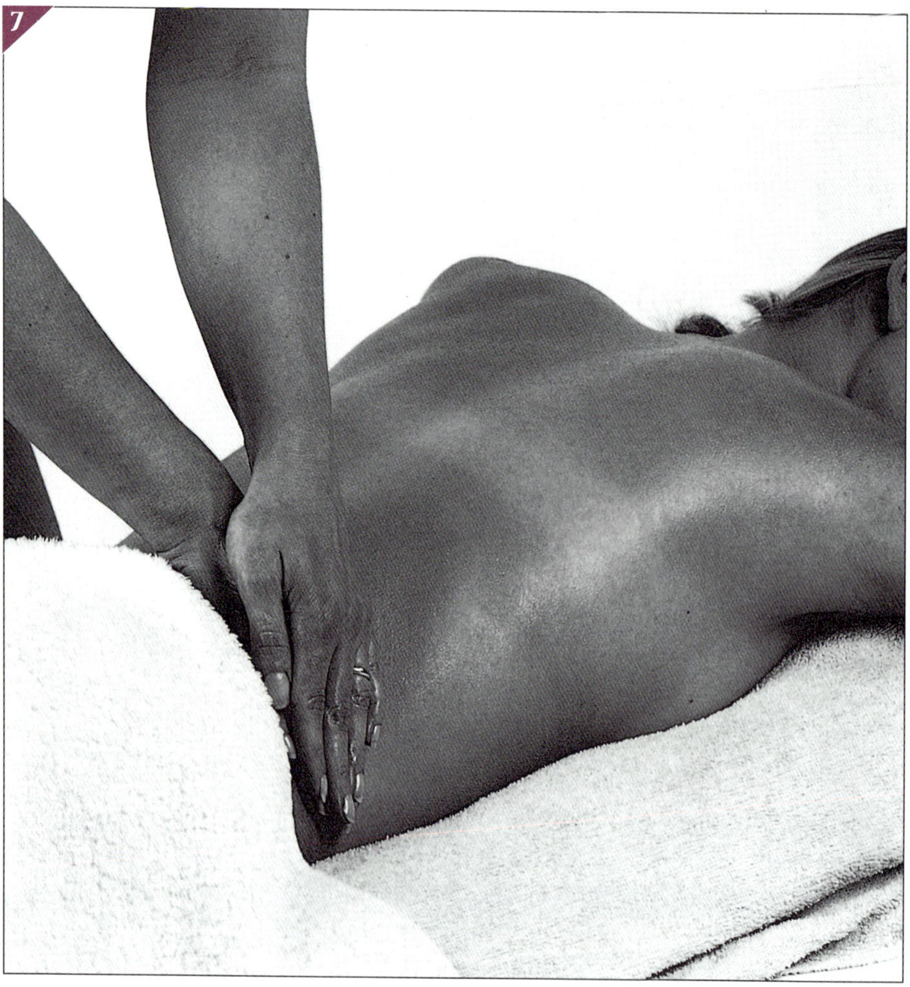

8 Move in an outward direction and open the fingers whilst the other hand comes underneath the top one and repeats the movement.

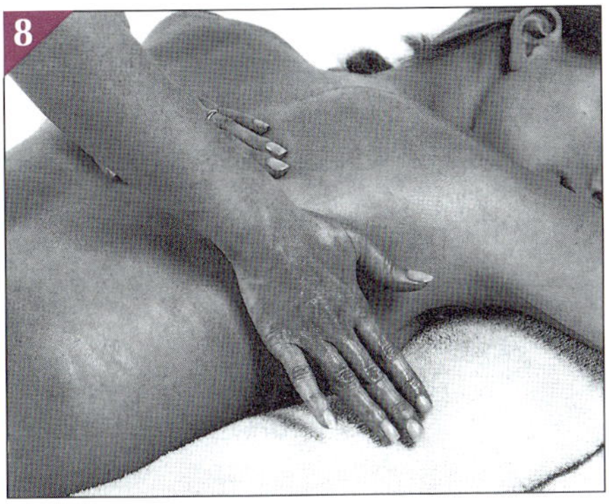

9 Each hand moves up the body a little and goes out like a fan. Repeat several times. Perform the same movement on the right-hand side of the back.

10 Time for effleurage, and then place one hand on top of the other at the left armpit level and, moving in a circular

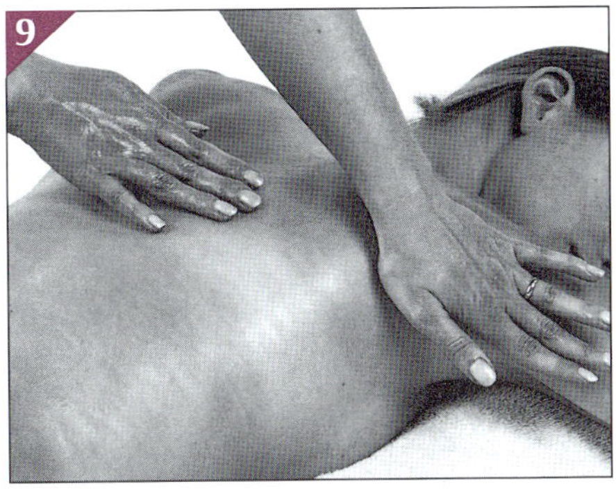

fashion, perform this movement on the side of the ribcage. Move lower down each time you make a circular movement with both hands. Finish at the buttock level, then transfer both hands to the side of the back and, starting from the right armpit level, perform circular movements with one hand on top of the other. Come down slowly at each consecutive circle, finishing on the right hip level.

Effleurage the whole area of the back, then cover the back with a warm towel and proceed with the leg massage.

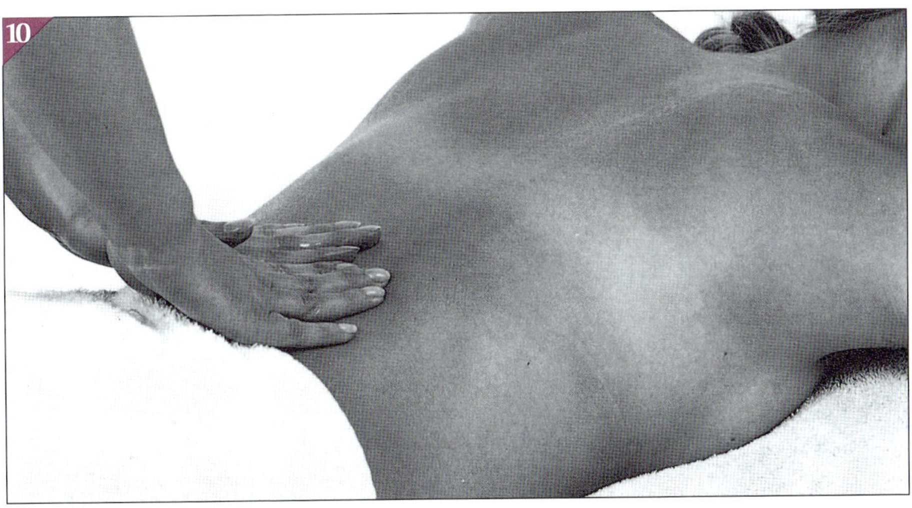

BACK OF LEGS

1 Spread the oil over the whole of the back of one leg with both your hands and effleurage firmly towards the thigh. Take the hand nearest to the top of the leg all the way up to the top of the thigh.

2 Take the hand nearest the feet to the back of the knee – alternate stroking one way only. Remember not to lose contact with the body between strokes. Repeat several times.

3 Stand at the side of the person being massaged and lift the foot up with one hand. Stroke it with the other hand, exerting some pressure from the ankle to the knee on the back of the leg.

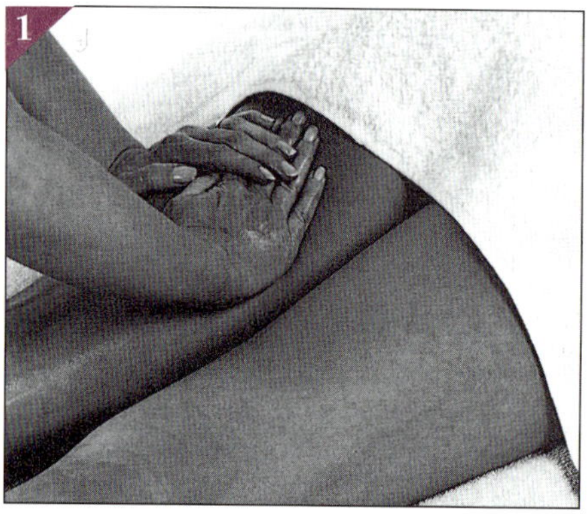

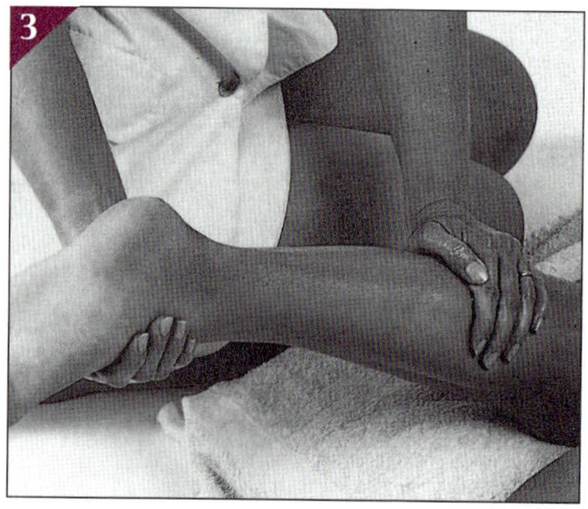

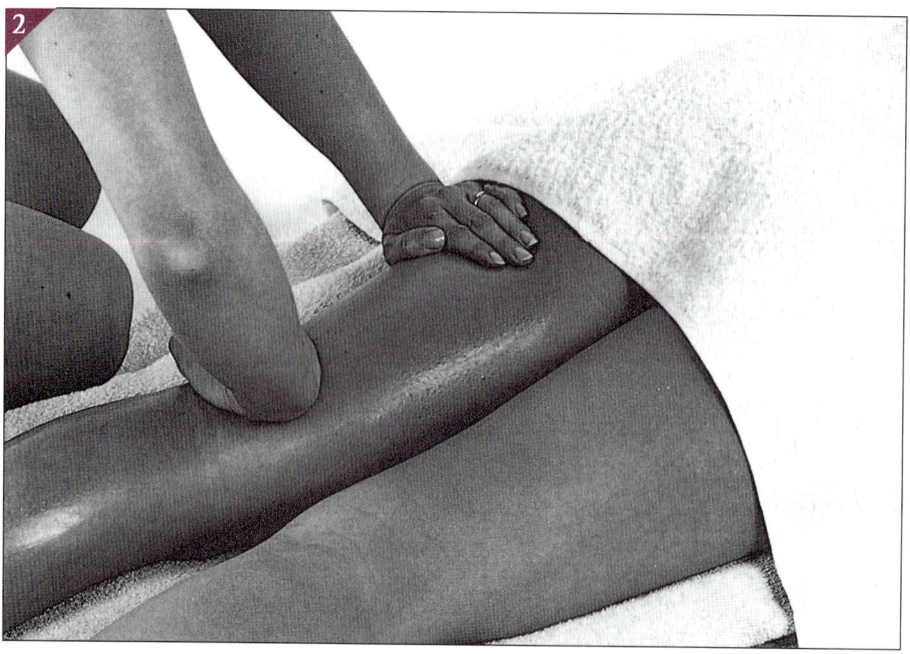

4
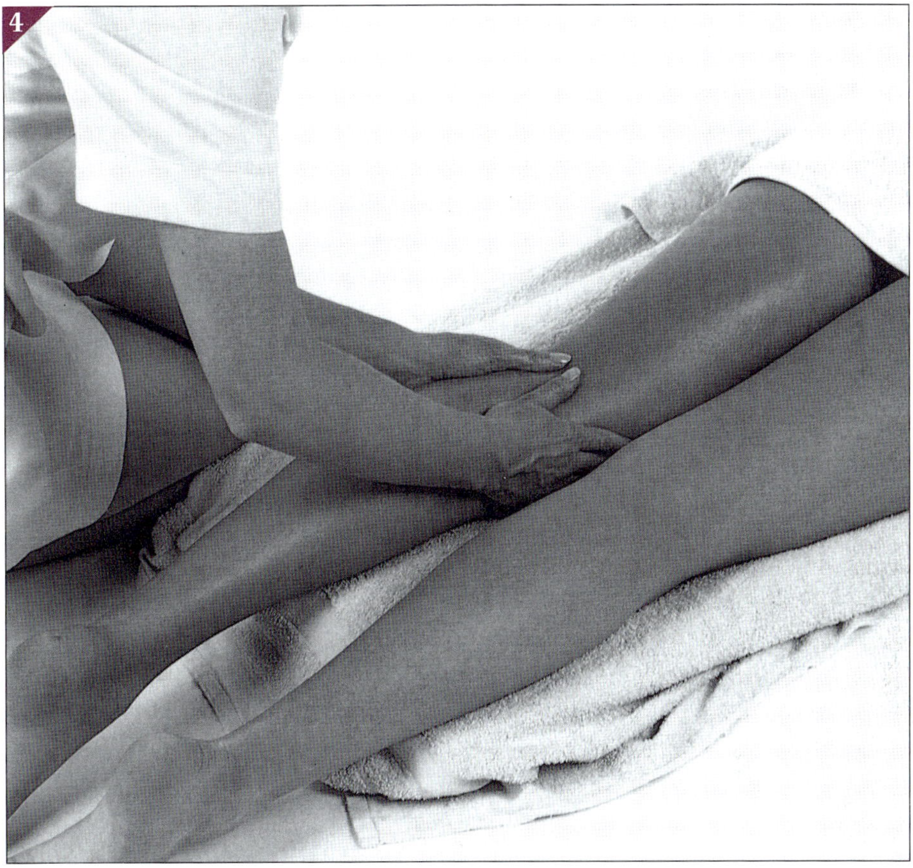

4 Keep the palm in the centre and the fingers relaxed around the leg. Repeat several times.

5 Working in a comfortable position, push the thumbs up the leg from the ankle to knee, coming back with a sliding movement or light effleurage down the sides of the legs.

5
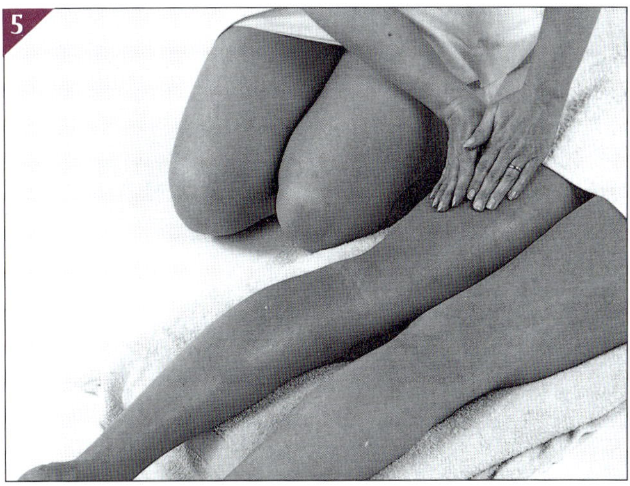

6 Position yourself at hip level of your model and place both hands at ankle level. Move the hands in light effleurage on both sides of the leg up to the hip level and lift one hand to place it on the ankle joint again whilst the other one finishes the movement on top of the leg. Join the top hand at ankle level with the other hand and perform continuous effleurage up to the top of the leg, parting the hands when the movement is finished in two stages so as not to lose the contact with the body. Repeat several times.

CONTRAINDICATIONS AND INDIVIDUAL BLENDS

Contraindications

There are several contraindications to aromatherapy massage.

- You need to make sure that the person being massaged has no fever.
- There should be no areas of bruising, infected skin or skin inflammation.
- Check the skin for recent scar tissue or any other skin disorder.
- Pregnancy or menstruation are contraindicated to aromatherapy treatment.
- Aromatherapy massage is not beneficial immediately after a steam bath or sauna.
- Post-stroke and diabetic patients need to be assessed very carefully.
- People on certain types of medication may display contraindications.

Individual blends

The blend of essential oils needs to suit the physical and emotional needs of the client and since each human being is an individual, people displaying the same symptoms may be massaged with many different essential oils. Aromatherapy is a holistic treatment and hence the blend will be prepared specifically to treat the unique needs of each client. The selection of an essential oil for aromatherapy massage will take into account the recipient's state of mind, personality and physical symptoms.

Arms

1 Gently effleurage the forearm in a resting position. Use one hand to perform the stroke while the other stabilizes this elongated part of the body. Lymph drainage receives direction by this application.

2 Hold the arm in the correct position for performing the gentle, upward friction. Perform this stroke on the forearm to aid the recipient's comfort and relaxation.

1
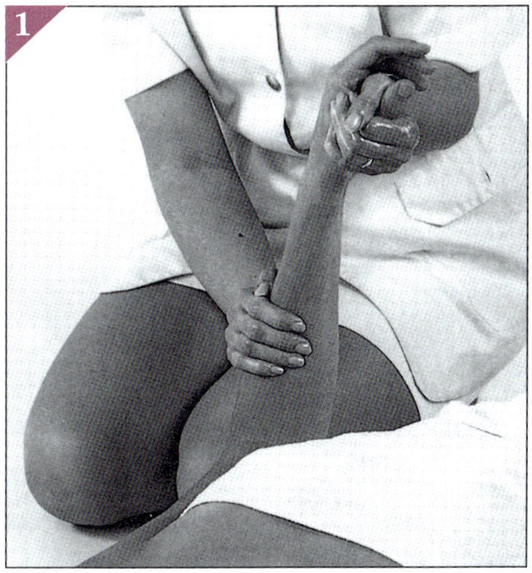

2
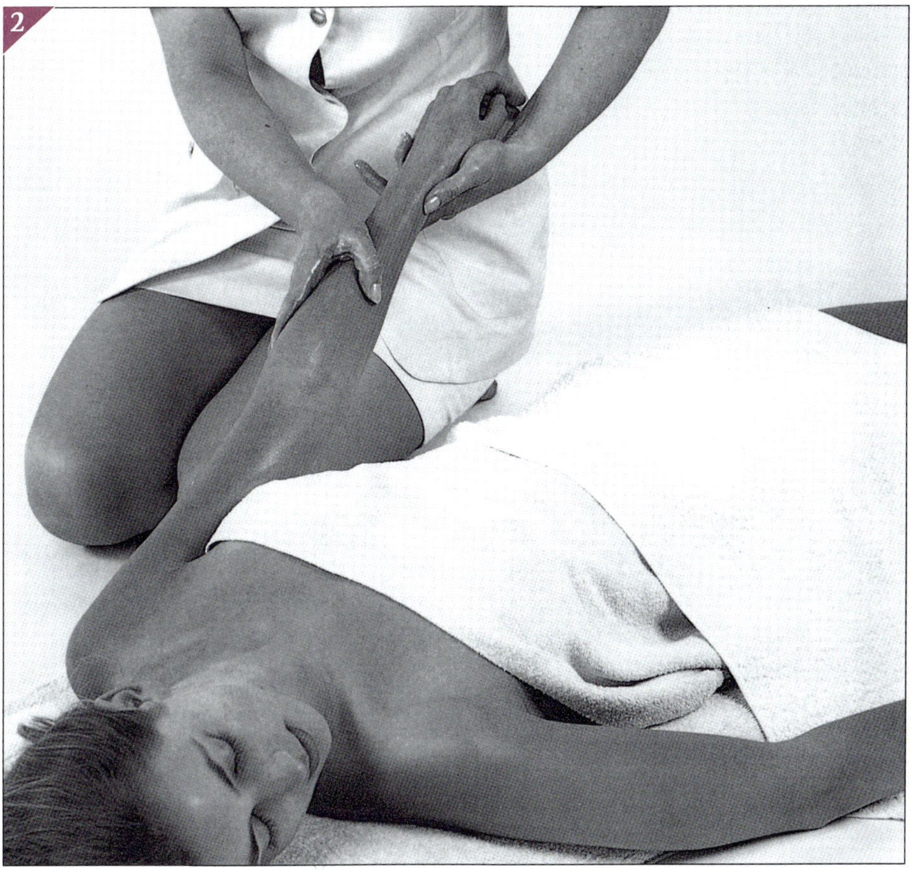

CHAPTER FIVE

MANUAL LYMPH DRAINAGE (MLD)

Manual Lymph Drainage is a type of massage which acts on the body's autonomic nervous system. The stress of everyday life and our polluted environment are contributing factors towards severe imbalances in the autonomic nervous system. This results in the sympathetic nervous system taking over.

Manual Lymph Drainage has a calming effect and restores balance within the nervous system. It should be performed in a rhythmical and slow sequence of movements to bring harmony and relaxation. In this way, it can promote growth and speedy recovery. In effect, Manual Lymph Drainage strengthens the body's ability to combat stress and restores peace and tranquillity. The achieved state of relaxation is the most important part of this treatment. With correct application, the relaxing effect produces a feeling of well-being which can lower or even eliminate pain sensation in the body.

Manual Lymph Drainage has a very specific action on the lymphatic system and indirectly on the immune system. It clears away the build up of toxins and this 'spring cleaning' in the body can then demonstrate itself in improved skin tone, texture and colour.

CONDITIONS IT CAN TREAT

- Conditions that react very favourably to Manual Lymph Drainage include skin conditions such as acne, particularly acne rosacea, dermatitis, facial oedema, chronic eczema, burns and allergies.
- Favourable results have been achieved in the treatment of keloids and cellulite.
- Heavy, tired and swollen legs react well to Manual Lymph Drainage.
- Weight reduction may be another benefit, due to surplus fluid being drained successfully. Lymph drainage combined with appropriately chosen physical exercise and diet may result in weight loss and maintenance.
- Premenstrual tension and headaches lend themselves very successfully to lymphatic drainage but the treatment should always be rendered by a fully qualified practitioner in this field.

FLUID RETENTION

The lower and upper limbs are very prone to fluid retention. The arms, particularly in women, are prone to congestions affecting the breast area, which very often result in breast tenderness and a general feeling of bloating. Fluid retention in the legs affects

Opposite: Manual Lymph Drainage restores balance to the nervous system.

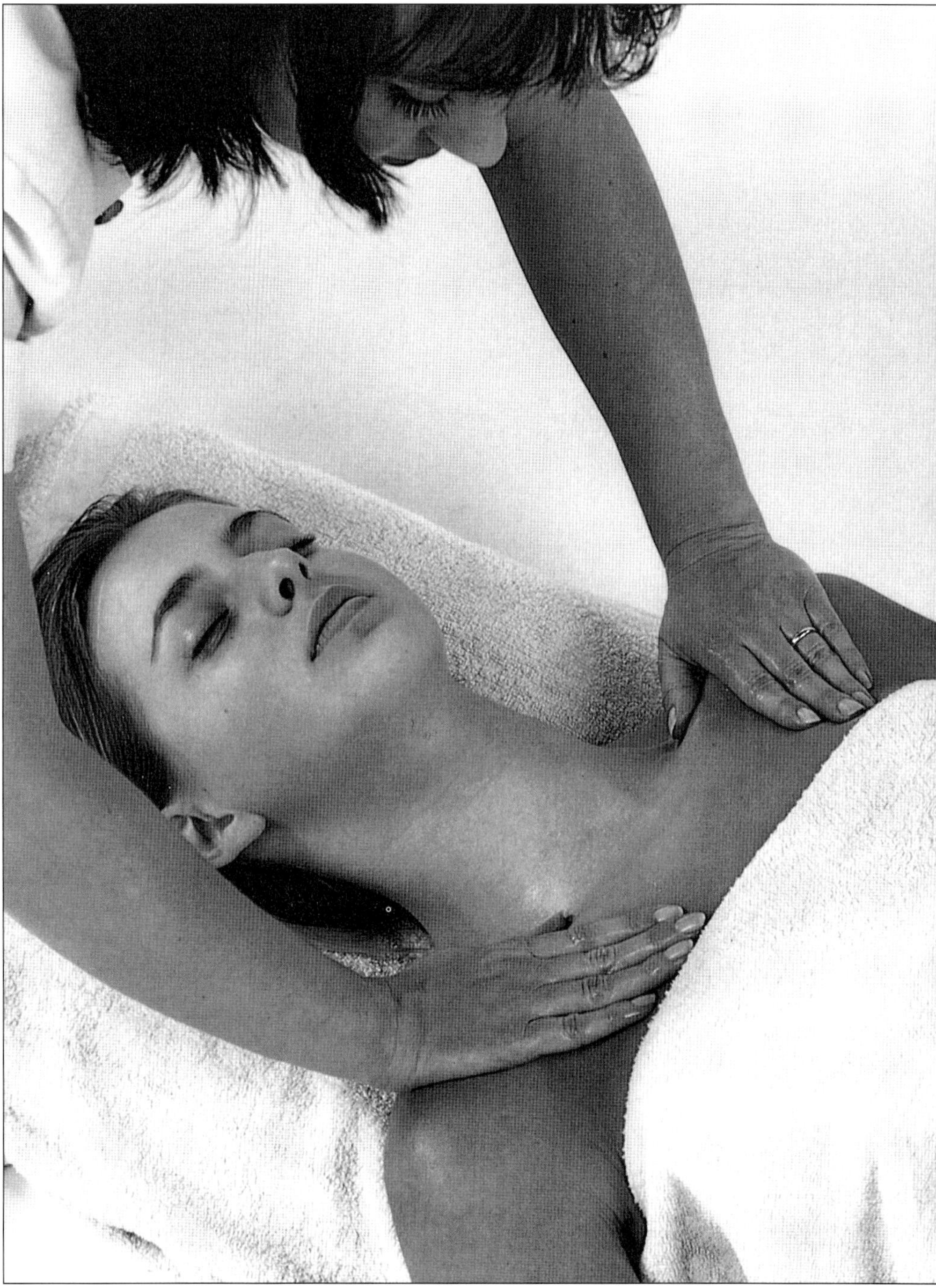

ORIGINS AND HISTORY

The history of the original method of Manual Lymph Drainage goes back to France to the year 1932. A Dr Vodder and his wife were working on the French Riviera treating many English patients with chronic colds caused by the inclement weather conditions in England. He developed his own way of treating these conditions by working directly on the lymph nodes, always with great success.

At that time, the lymphatic system was not emphasised in the training of natural therapists and not even deeply understood by the medical profession. However, Vodder's method was so successful that he published the results of his work in Paris, in 1936. He originated the term 'Manual Lymph Drainage' (MLD). The Society for Dr Vodder's MLD was founded in 1967, and in 1976 it was integrated into the German Society of Lymphology. Also, in 1972, the Society for Dr Vodder's Lymph Drainage in Walchsee was established in order to preserve his work and his teaching methods.

Vodder's technique of Manual Lymph Drainage is not easy to learn. In order to achieve good results, the application of this method has to be very specific. If applied correctly, Manual Lymph Drainage can reduce oedema through the lymph vessels and relieve pain and discomfort. It has a calming effect on the recipient and it relaxes the hypertonus of the skeletal muscles by a series of rhythmical and slow movements.

This therapeutic treatment very often produces rapid results not only in cosmetic and preventative measures but also in treating specific disorders in the body. In recent years, the medical profession has begun to realise the importance of the lymphatic system in connection with the onset of physical illnesses. It was the effect of the physiological functions of the lymphatic system on the body's defence mechanism that made the Manual Lymph Drainage treatment so popular. The growth of the research field into the defence mechanism in the immune system put Manual Lymph Drainage in a prominent position among the natural tactile therapies.

We live in the world of bacteria and viruses and, although tiny in appearance, they are our deadly enemies. They strike with the speed of lightning and the aftermath in the body caused by their deadly accuracy of attack destroys the natural defences within the immune system. The gradual weakening of the defence mechanism causes the body to fall ill for long periods at a time and the chances of recovery each time they strike are lower and slower.

the ankles and can be treated successfully with Manual Lymph Drainage.

Manual Lymph Drainage relieves pain, normalizes muscle tone and also relaxes the hypertonicity of the skeletal muscles. Due to its diverse effects, Manual Lymph Drainage finds many uses and treats many conditions with lymphostatic oedema. The age of the patient, type of illness and the chronicity will play an important role in opting for lymph individual drainage. In each case, depending on its merits, the lymph drainage may be applied slightly differently, and the duration and frequency of treatment may differ from one case history to another.

ACHIEVING THE BEST RESULTS

To achieve the best results with Manual Lymph Drainage, you must analyse the environment in which it will be applied and the type of complaint that it is being used to treat.

- The room should be at a comfortable temperature.
- The person being treated should be in a comfortable position and undisturbed by light or sound.
- The therapist should have warm hands and the pressure exerted during treatment must feel pleasant and relaxing without causing any reddening of the skin.
- A drop of lubricant, such as vegetable oil, may be used if the body is covered in thick hair or the skin surface is very dry.
- The duration of the first session should not last more than 10 to 15 minutes.

Below: Manual Lymph Drainage should be performed behind the recipient.

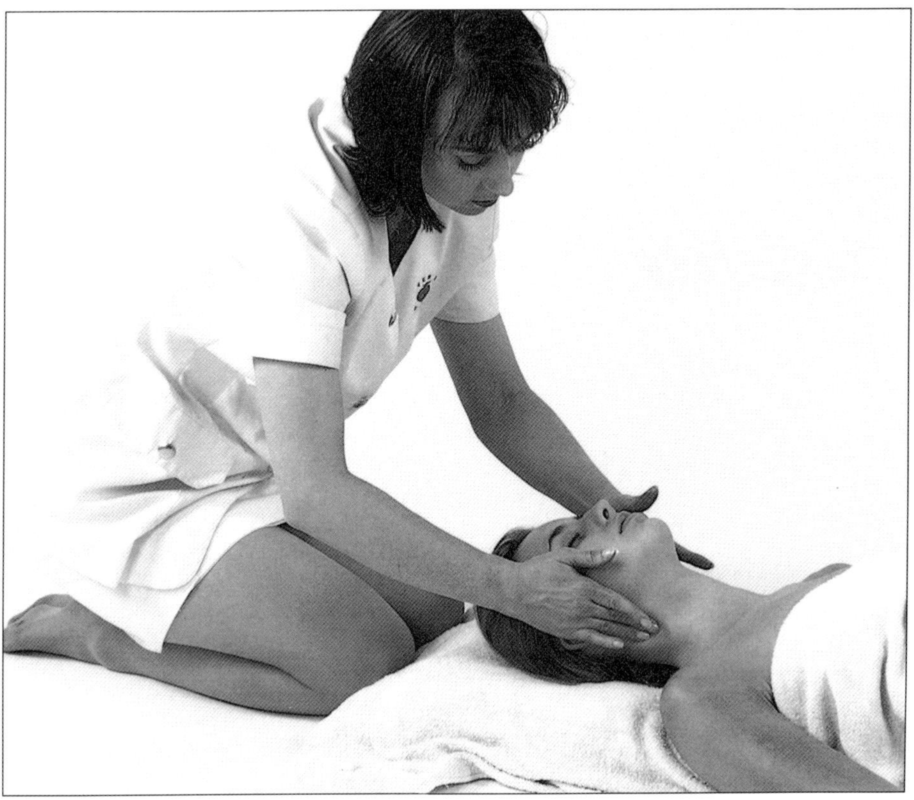

SIMPLE MLD TECHNIQUES

THE NECK AND SHOULDERS

1 With the person being massaged lying down in a supine position (on the back, facing the ceiling), apply effleurage with several fan-shaped strokes with the thumbs from the sternum towards the armpits.

2 The last stroke should follow the line of the person's clavicle (collar bone).

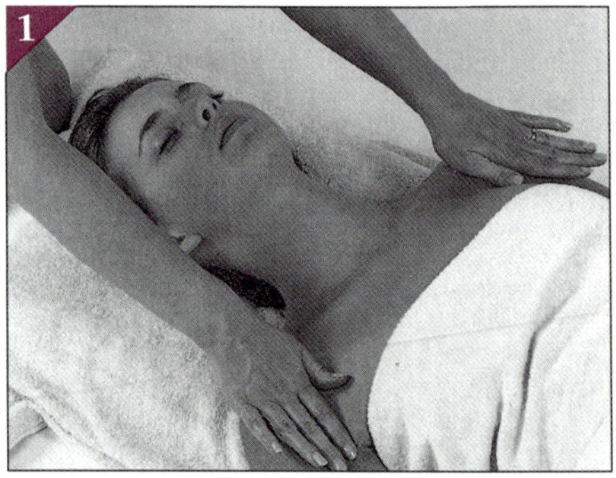

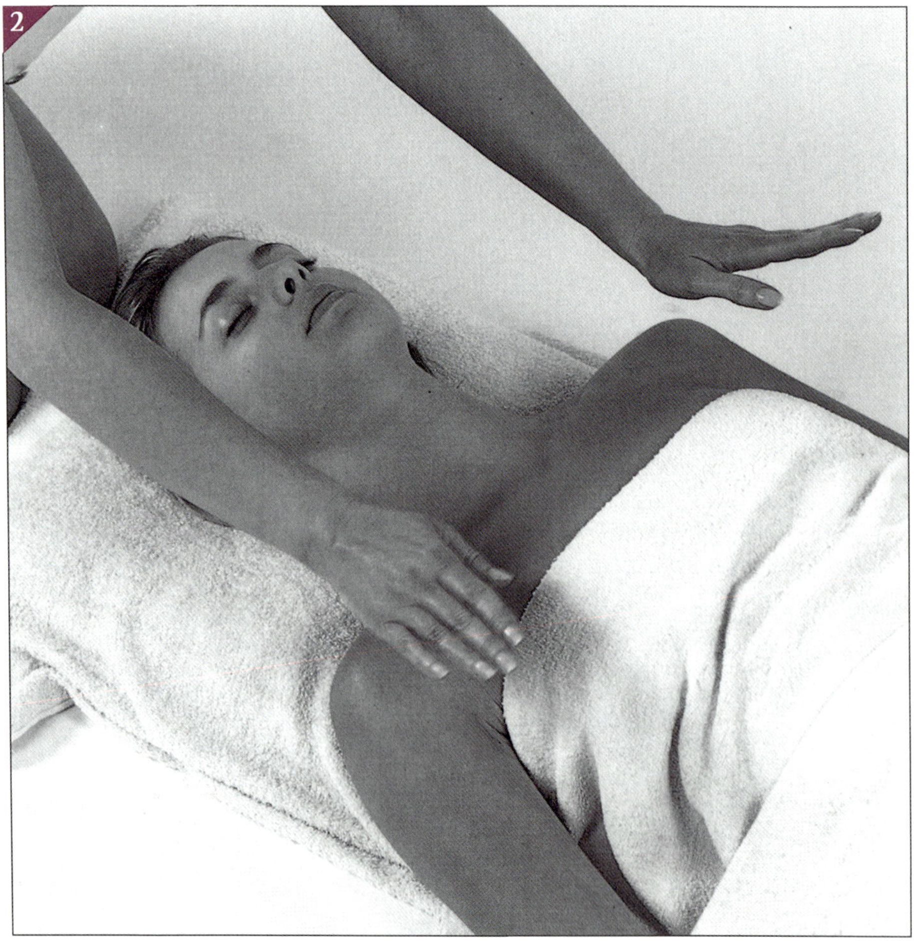

3 Apply several stationary circles over the lymph nodes at the side of the neck in three stages, coming down each time. This is necessary to facilitate drainage of the cervical lymph nodes.

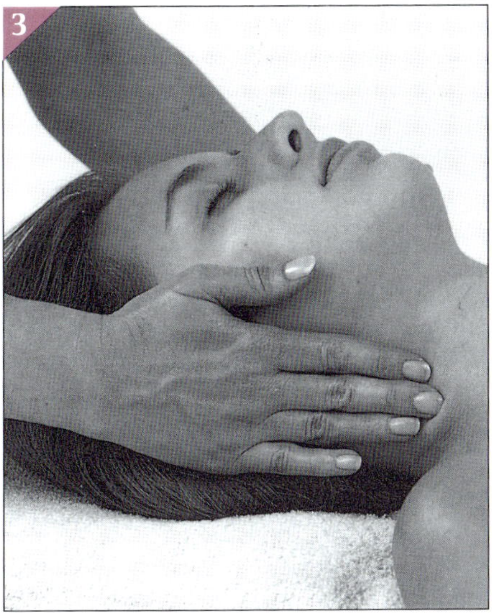

4 To drain the occiput, perform stationary circles beginning at the base of the skull, following the cervical vertebrae and finishing above the clavicle.

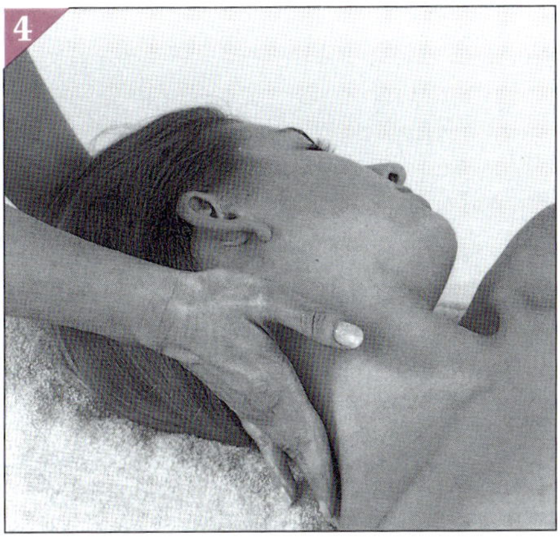

5 Follow by stationary circles from the tip of the chin to the angle of the jaw.

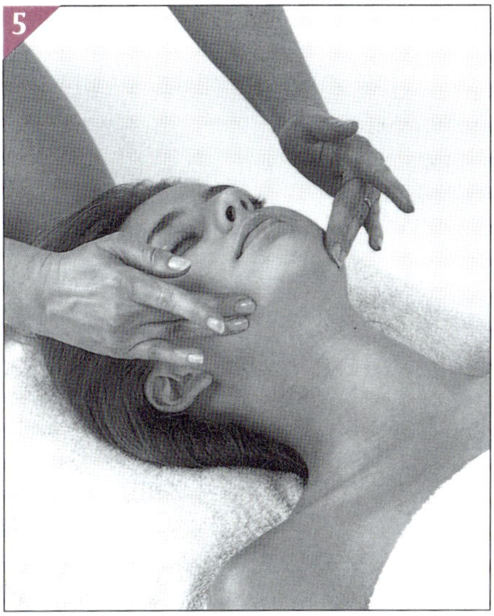

6 Move down each time towards the clavicle at the terminus point.

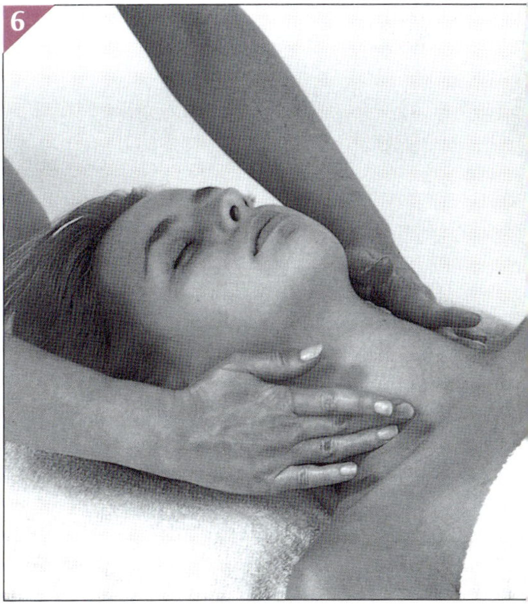

7 Now apply several stationary circles in front of and behind the ears of the person who is receiving Manual Lymph Drainage, finishing at the same point of the clavicle (collar bone).

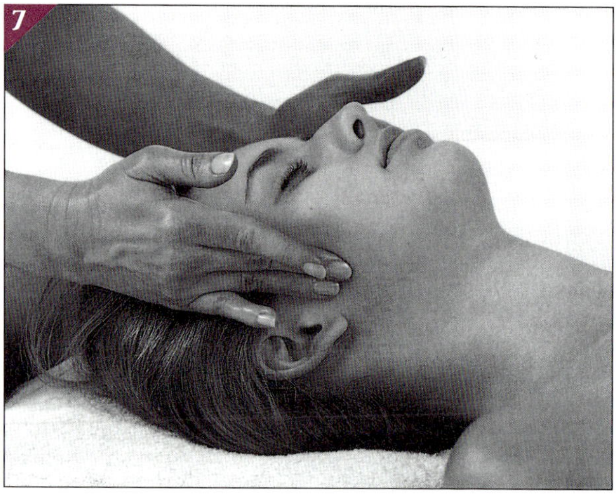

8 Now, move your hand on to the recipient's shoulder, over the ball of the shoulder.

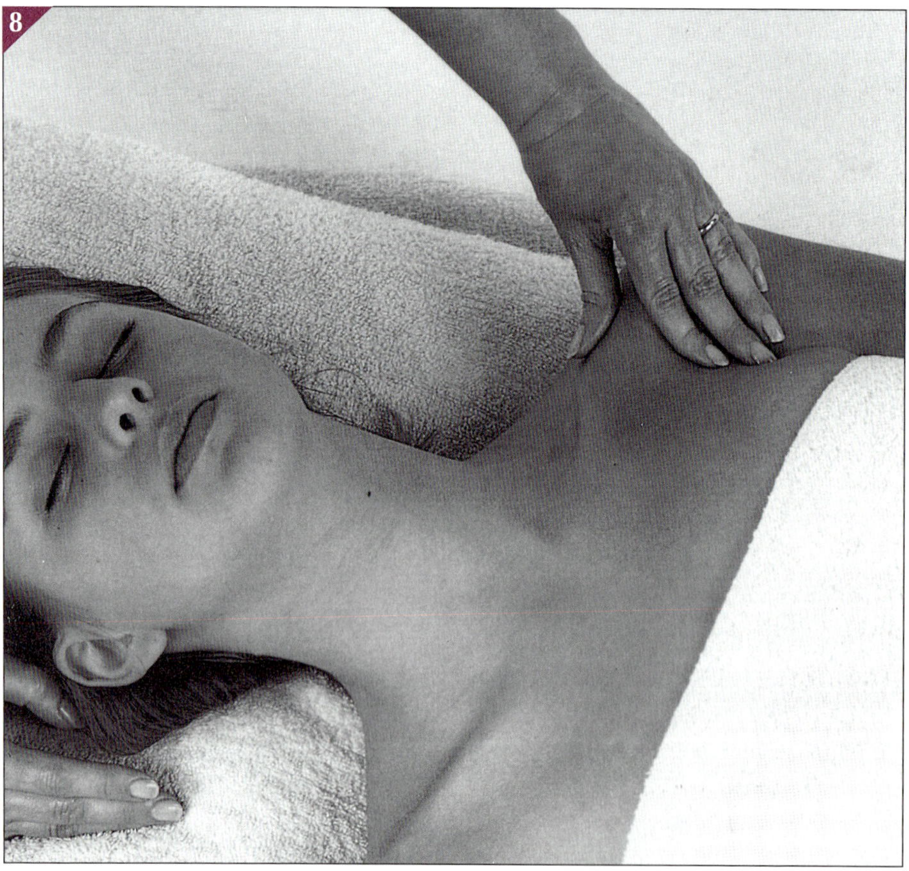

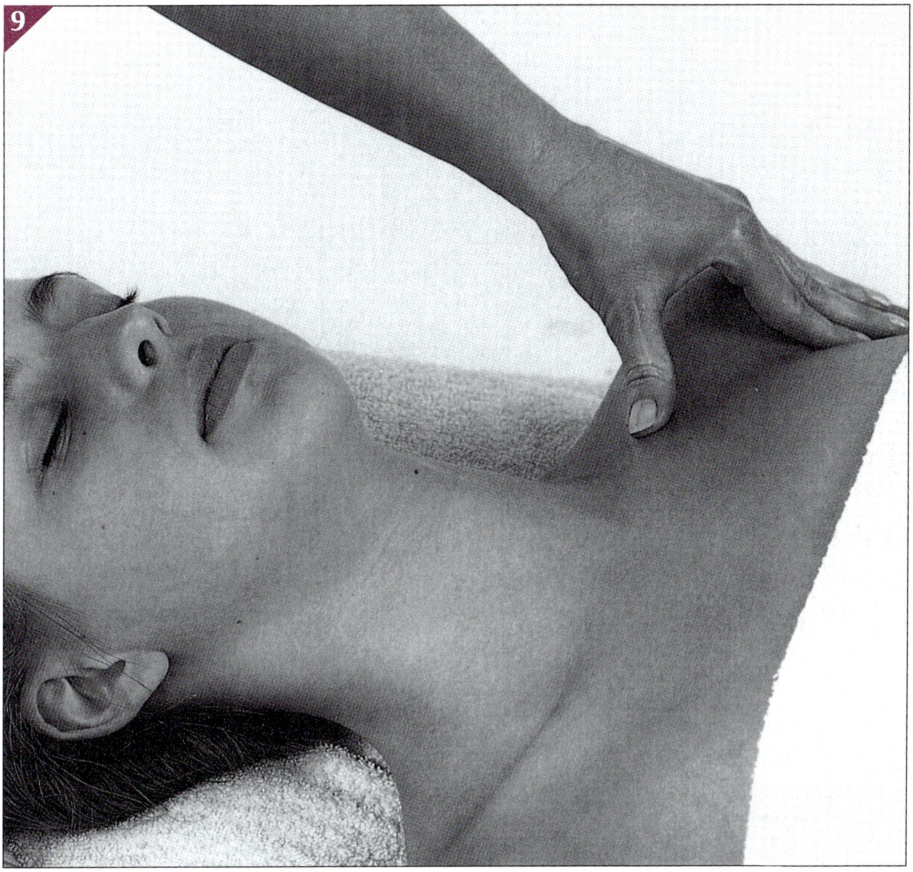

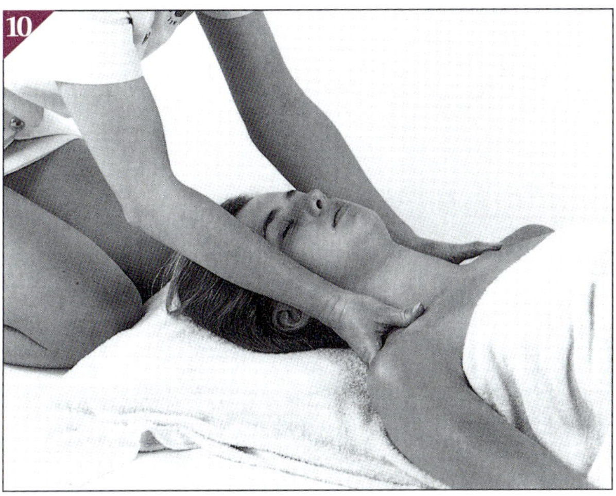

9 Proceed with some stationary circles on the border of the trapezius muscle and the terminus.

10 Start again at the ball of the shoulder, with some stationary circles above the clavicle (shoulder blade) and then finish at the terminus point.

11 This sequence can be finished with light effleurage of the whole area of the neck and shoulder joint from the top of the neck to the armpit.

12 Place your fingers at the back of the neck, with the thumbs on the front of the neck. It is a very relaxing and soothing stroke which is extremely calming and creates the feeling of well-being and tranquillity.

Note: the movements used in Manual Lymph Drainage have to be slow, continuous and rhythmical. It is important to retain the fluency of the strokes throughout the sequence. This technique should be practised several times in order to achieve these characteristics, but the effect is always of peace and serenity for the recipient and therapist alike.

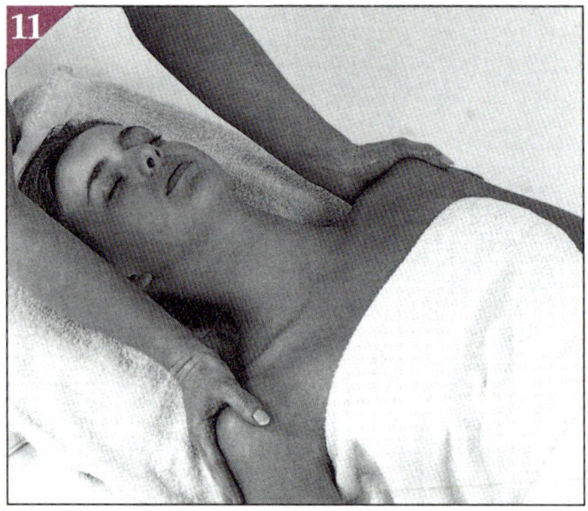

CONTRAINDICATIONS

There are several contraindications to Manual Lymph Drainage and these should be observed before commencing treatment.

In general terms, the contraindications would include the following.

- Some cancer cases.
- People suffering from asthma and bronchitis (the treatment could precipitate an attack).
- Tuberculosis.
- Menstruation (if Manual Lymph Drainage is performed on the abdomen as well as other body parts).
- Low blood pressure.
- Any type of inflammatory conditions with pain and discomfort.

BENEFITS OF MANUAL LYMPH DRAINAGE

The benefits of this treatment are multifold. Manual Lymph Drainage is often extremely effective for treating skin conditions such as acne, eczema and psoriasis. It can counteract the frequency of headaches, migraines, allergic reactions, colds and even facial paralysis. It can also be very successful in treating arthritic conditions, gout, sinusitis and tonsillitis, loss of hair and stress.

Manual Lymph Drainage acts very specifically on the fluid level in the body and hence this treatment is of great value to fluid retention sufferers. It can help fight cellulite and contribute to weight loss. This is good news for slimmers, who can sustain weight loss if they combine Manual Lymph Drainage treatment with a good diet and some appropriate exercise.

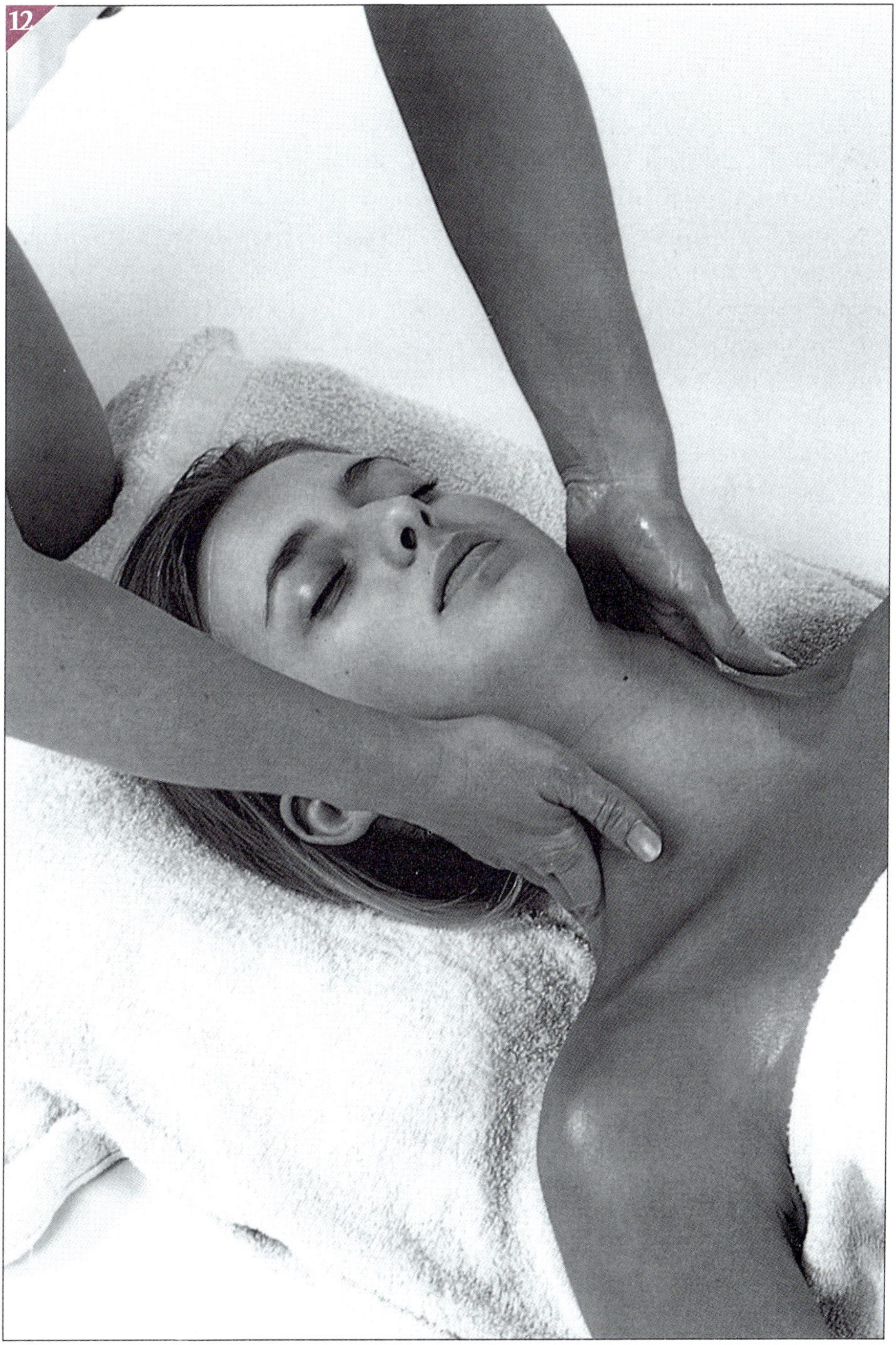
12

6

BABY MASSAGE

During my travels in India and Nepal, I observed mothers looking after their babies. The close relationship between a mother and her baby continues for a long time and this closeness is emphasised by touch. Babies sleep with their mothers and are massaged every day. In Africa and South America, many infants are regularly massaged by their parents and other family members for many months after birth.

In Western societies, the tactile contact between the mother and baby is usually short-lived and amounts only to personal contact at the time of feeding and changing nappies. Colic is usually treated with gripe water and other ailments by antibiotics and

Below: baby massage not only helps bonding between the mother and baby but also promotes health and growth.

painkillers. The personal and direct contact with a baby born in hospital may take the form of handling by the mother and the hospital staff for feeding purposes, bringing up wind and changing nappies. Personal attention and frequent touch, such as massage, are labour-intensive and financial restraints in the field of health care prohibit this prolonged one-to-one treatment in the hospital environment.

THE IMPORTANCE OF TOUCH

Touch is very important to human beings – touch is healing, and healing is touch. The most recent research studies confirm that massage promotes growth and behavioural benefits in infants.

■ Babies who are massaged regularly display alertness and spend more time absorbed in activities during their waking hours.

■ These babies cry less and suffer lower stress levels.

■ They gain weight faster because their digestive system works more efficiently.

■ They perform better in the assessment levels of temperament and emotional behaviour.

■ When we look at the 'mechanical' level of the benefits of massage, massaged babies often display better presentation in the musculoskeletal, nervous and circulatory systems. This is usually demonstrated by significantly reduced levels of anxiety and distress (colic-prone babies tend to suffer less discomfort).

■ Massage improves circulation and helps to relieve colic and constipation.

■ Massage induces a state of relaxation and enhances alertness for the activities in the babies' prolonged 'awake' state.

■ Their sleep pattern is more regular and uninterrupted which, in turn, leads to greater relaxation resulting in quieter predispositions.

■ Massage eases tense muscles and helps the baby to cope with pain. Even if pain occurs, the massaged baby has a greater ability to withstand it.

In other words, massage helps to protect the infant's body from distress. Since stress causes illness, this, in turn, protects the infant from illness. Dr Tiffany Field from the Miami Touch Research Institute is one of the leading exponents of infant massage and has done a great deal of research and evaluation of its clinical value. The

BENEFITS OF INFANT MASSAGE

■ Massage promotes health and happiness and enhances the bonding process and mutual love between parents and their children.

■ Regularly massaged babies display lesser susceptibility to colds, sickness and diarrhoea.

■ Stroking the abdomen can ease wind and colic, and massaging the baby's legs and arms promotes stronger joints.

■ When massaged before bedtime, babies sleep more soundly which is very helpful to mothers – they too can relax at night.

examination of the 'biology of touch' has initiated a series of wide-ranging studies in tactile experience and child healthcare.

Preparation for massage

Baby massage should be performed in a loving and comfortable atmosphere. The room should be quiet, warm and draught-free. Enough support should be to hand, i.e. cushions, pillows or a mattress. Clean, warm towels should be at the ready and massage oil within easy reach. Soft music and subdued lighting would be an added boon to your session of baby massage.

Carrier and essential oils

The massage oil should ideally be of vegetable origin, e.g. Sweet Almond, Grapeseed, Sunflower or Apricot kernel oil. These oils are light and nourishing to the skin and do not block the pores. Scented oil may be used, but natural essential oils are preferable to the synthetic perfumes since they can irritate the baby's skin.

The massage oil should be kept in a vessel such as a saucer or an eggcup. If you decide to use an essential oil, put one or two drops of, say, Chamomile or Lavender oil, into the eggcup or a saucer and mix the blend with your finger. Ensure that the massage oil is warm.

Safety checklist

Before we start the massage, we need to go over the safety checklist.

■ Only babies in good health should be massaged – if in doubt, you should consult your doctor first.

■ Unstable joints, skin infections, skin rashes, eczema or any other broken skin should be investigated beforehand.

■ The after-effects of vaccinations may preclude a baby being massaged.

■ Babies on medication may carry the contraindication to massage as well.

A few words of warning

■ Do not pour the oil directly on to the skin.

■ Do not place the container on a radiator or any other source of heat.

■ Do not apply the oil to the baby's face; it may irritate the eyes.

■ Do not undress the baby completely. Accidents do happen, particularly when babies are being massaged, and this could interrupt your routine and spoil your massage sequence and fluency of strokes. Take the nappy off only when you have finished the head, chest and the legs, and are ready to massage the abdomen.

Prepare yourself

■ Wear loose, comfortable clothes.

■ Your fingernails should be short.

■ Don't wear jewellery during treatment.

■ Your hair should be tied back.

■ Now take a few slow, deep breaths, relax your shoulders, warm up your hands and concentrate on the forthcoming activities.

Opposite: the relationship between mother and baby can be enhanced by regular baby massage.

THE MASSAGE

Place the baby securely on a towel on your lap, but you may feel more comfortable if you kneel on a cushion with your baby on the towel on the floor. In this case you will have to learn to lean forwards from the hips rather than curve your back. Use your hip joints to avoid backache. It is best to begin with your baby facing you so that you can keep eye contact during this session and also give encouragement by using your voice – talking or even singing to your baby. It will also help you to assess the baby's reactions to your touch.

THE HEAD

1 You may decide to begin by stroking the head ever so gently, moving gradually from the top of the head to the base of the skull, with both hands on the same level during this movement. This will be very soothing and reassuring to the baby.

2 Support your baby's head between your hands and, using the pads of your thumbs, perform gentle effleurage from just above the bridge of the nose, upward towards the hairline.

THE CHEST

1 Start with both hands together in the middle of the ribcage. Gently move both hands

Below: begin the chest massage by moving the hands from the middle to the sides of the baby's chest.

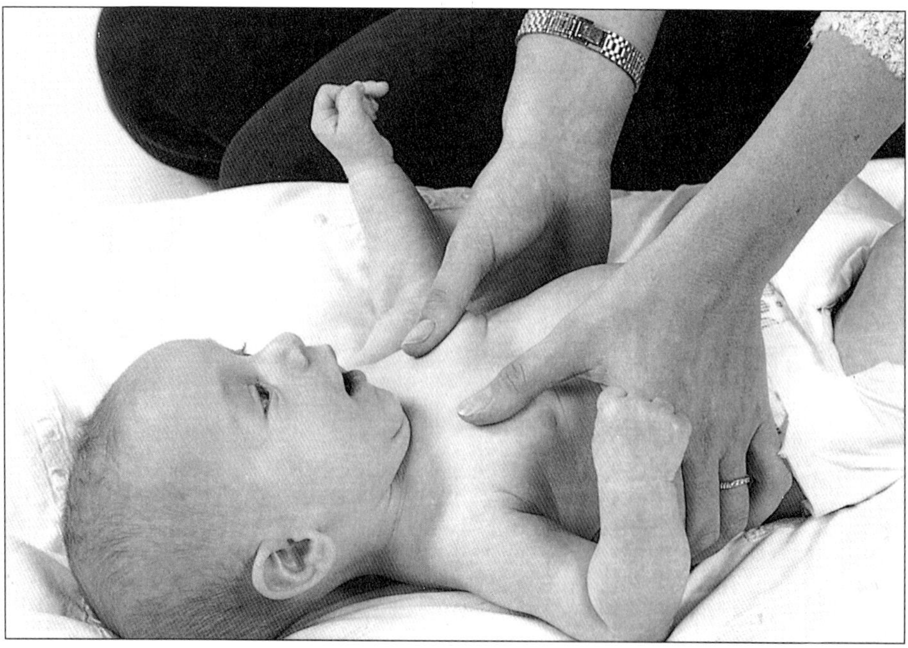

to the sides of the chest. Slide them back to the starting point without any pressure this time but not losing contact with the body, and then effleurage to the sides again.

2 On the return movement, place both hands slightly lower down each time you effleurage so that you cover the whole area of the chest. Since the ribcage is only small, this will possibly only take two or three steps of the effleurage stroke.

3 With both hands placed stationary at the bottom of the breastbone, move the pads of your thumbs in small circles up, out and over the collarbone, finishing with effleurage down the arms.

Below: when massaging the baby's legs, use gentle stroking and squeezing movements.

The legs

1 Apply the oil with gentle effleurage, using long, firm upward strokes.

2 Massage each leg individually by stroking up to the hips and handling the flesh between your fingers and the thumb when going down. This has a 'squeezing' effect all the way to the toes.

3 Handling the foot gently, rotate it slowly and effleurage thoroughly with either one or both hands.

4 With your thumb, effleurage gently the sole of the baby's foot from the heel up to the toes.

5 Squeeze each of the baby's toes ever so gently and carefully.

6 Effleurage the full length of the leg and then repeat the sequence on the baby's other leg.

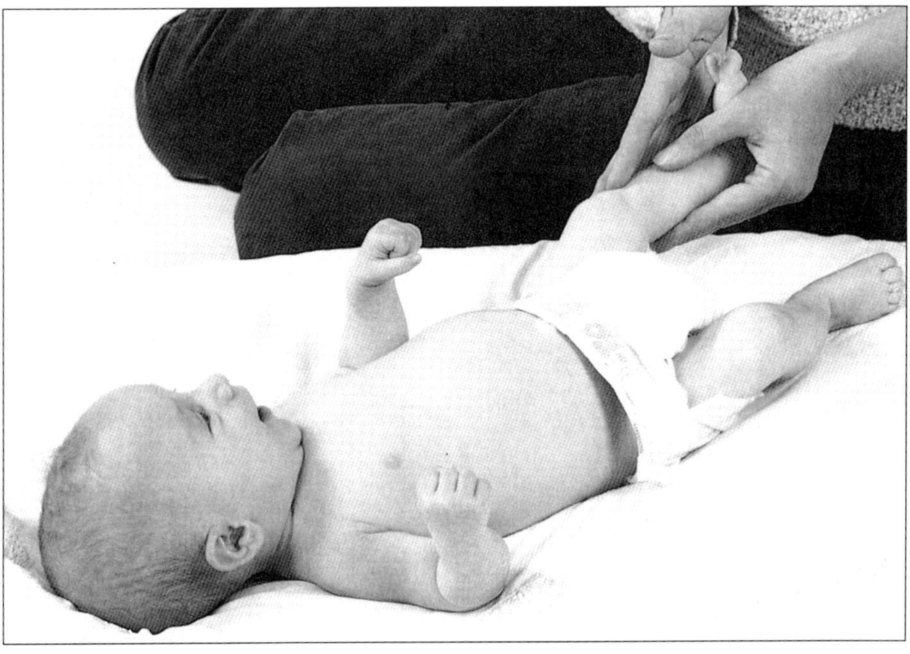

THE ABDOMEN

1 The baby's tummy is a very sensitive area. Therefore only a very gentle touch is needed here.

2 Move your hands to the sides of your baby's tummy and pause a while.

3 Slowly stroke the tummy in a clockwise direction. Keep in contact with the body and avoid the area around the navel if it has not healed properly.

4 Rest your hand on the pubic bone with outstretched fingers facing the baby's head and gently move the fingers from the right to the left side of the baby's abdomen. Repeat several times.

5 Effleurage with care and then replace the baby's nappy.

Below: use a gentle touch on the sensitive abdominal area.

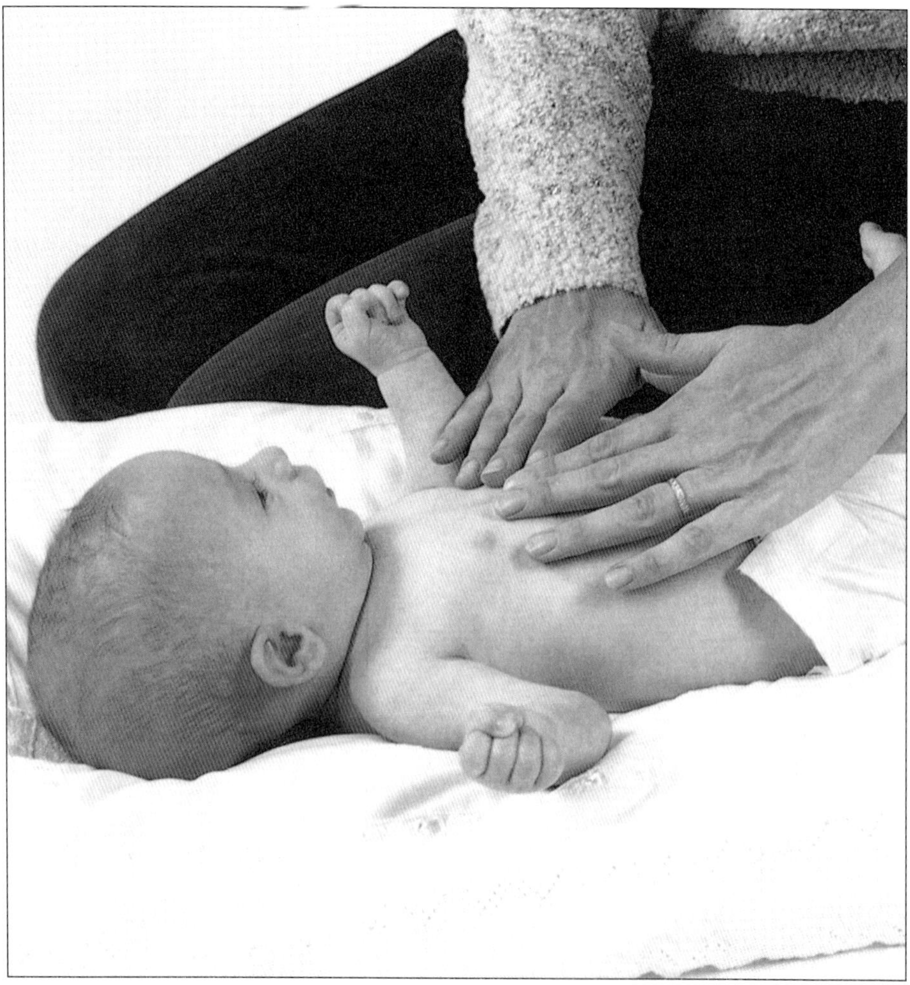

THE ARMS

1 They need to be massaged one at a time. Support the arms with one hand and, using thumb circles, apply the oil on the upper arm between the elbow and armpit.

2 Effleurage the full length of the arm again.

3 Handle the baby's lower arm in your hand and apply firm effleurage.

4 Massage the palm of the hand with your thumb and then individually each finger of the baby's hand.

5 Apply even, firm and slow effleurage on the full length of the arm again and then perform the same sequence of movements on the other arm.

6 Cover the baby in a warm towel.

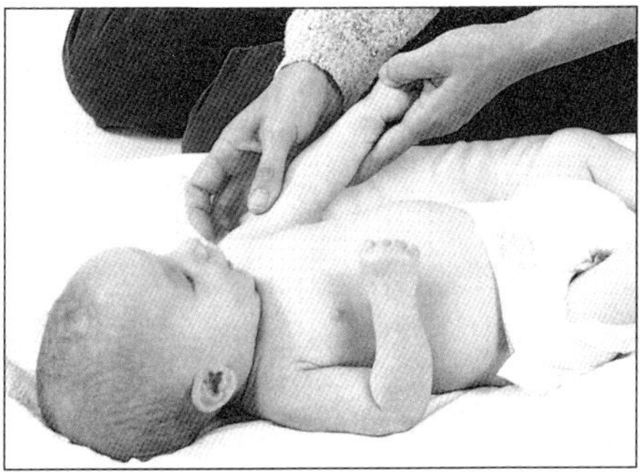

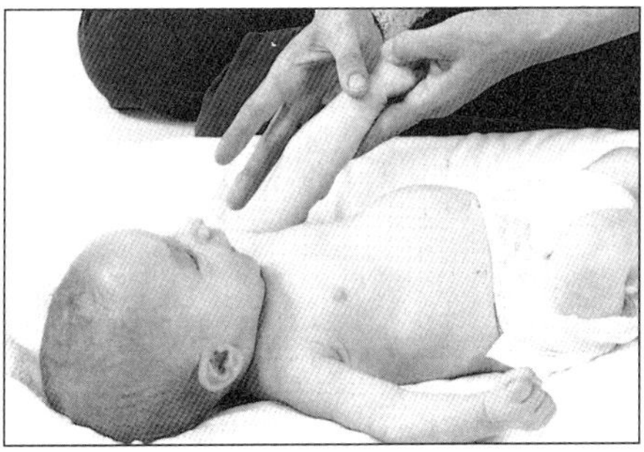

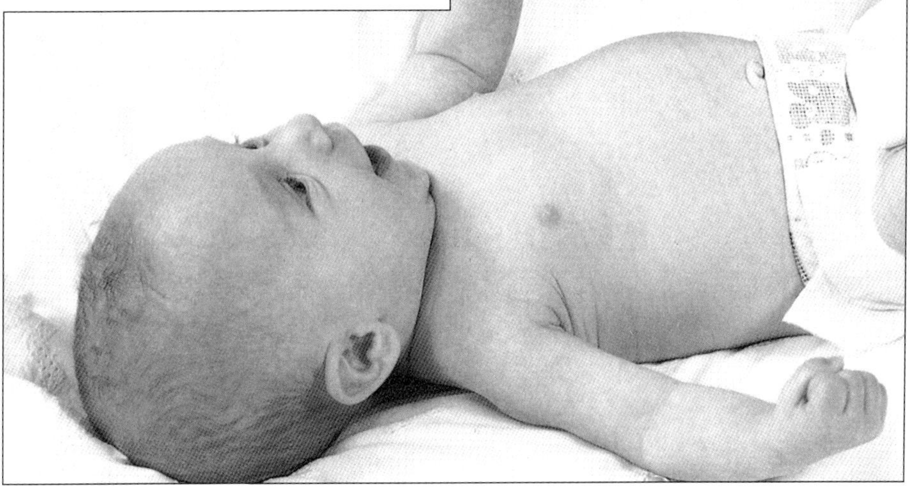

Left: apply oil and then gently stroke the baby's arms.
Below left: now apply firmer effleurage movements to the arms.
Below: massage the baby's fingers.

THE BACK

1 Singing or talking, turn your baby on to the tummy. If necessary, place a rolled towel under the chest.

2 Apply some oil to the buttocks and back, using a long, rhythmical effleurage movement, with one hand following the other one.

3 Place both hands at the bottom of the spine and perform small circles with your fingertips on either side of the spine.

4 Come down with an effleurage stroke with no pressure.

5 Move outwards all the way to the sides of the buttocks with a larger circular movement.

6 Apply gentle effleurage with one or both hands up the whole of the back to the shoulder and, without stopping, effleurage the arm to the hand and fingers.

7 On the way down, run your hand down each leg until you reach the foot. Gently rub the baby's toes just before you lose contact with the body to indicate the end of your massage sequence.

8 You may decide to finish the back with feathering; this gentle stroke is much loved by infants of all ages.

9 Cover the baby in a warm towel and cuddle him/her. Stay quiet for a few moments with the baby in your arms.

Below: if wished, support the chest and shoulders with a rolled towel but ensure the baby is comfortable and there is no danger of suffocation.

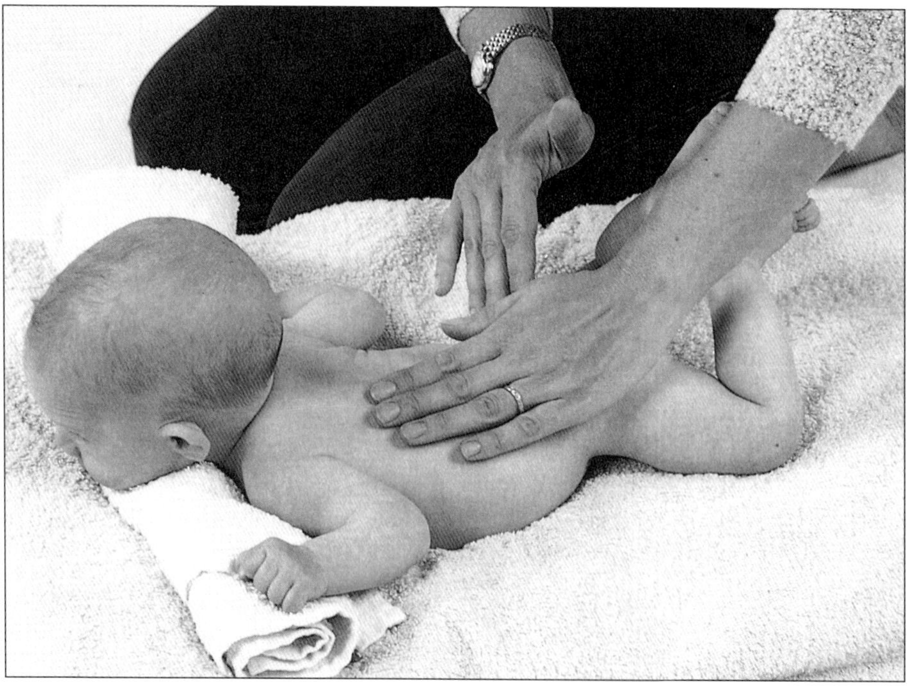

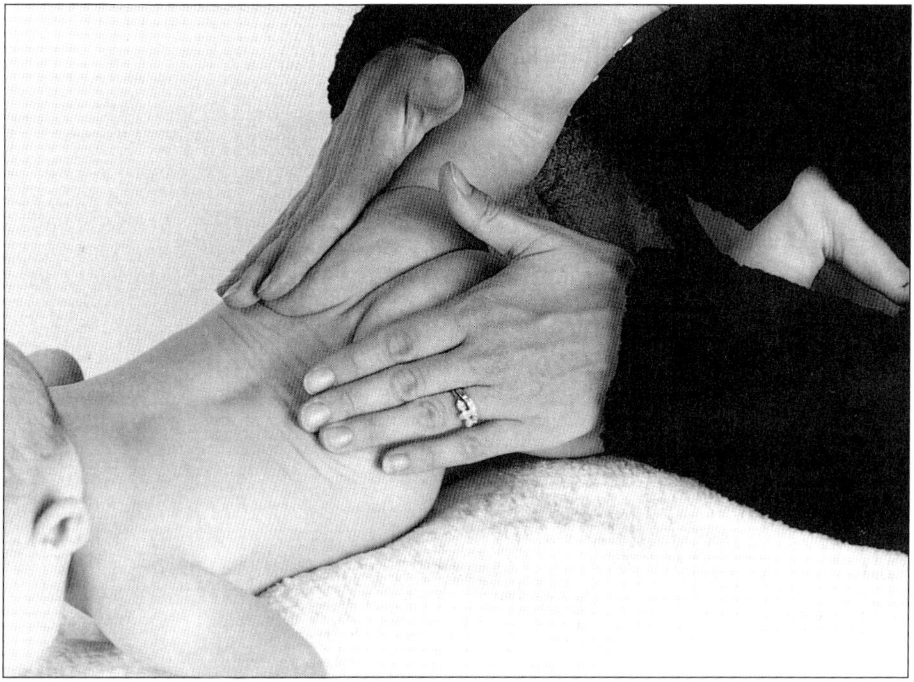

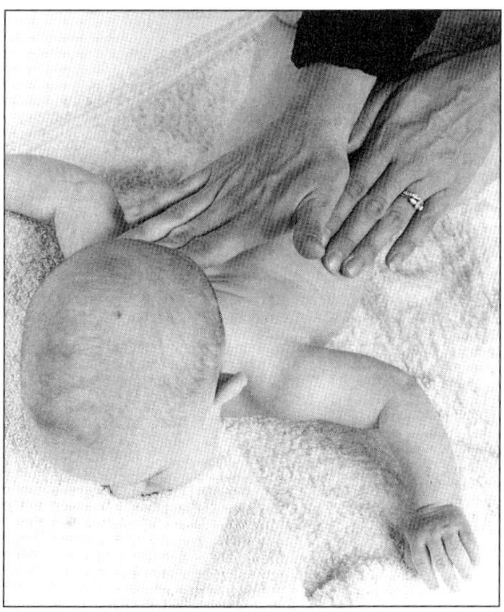

Above: finish the massage with some gentle effleurage or feathering to relax and soothe your baby.

Above: apply gentle effleurage movements to the baby's back.

SUMMARY

Hopefully your massage will help your baby's breathing and boost the immune system. His/her skin will improve because massage helps to eliminate waste products and toxins. Your baby should benefit from your massage by developing suppleness of the muscles and joints. The massage should aid digestion, relieve colic and prevent constipation. Your little infant should be able to sleep like an angel and let you relax at the same time. If you enjoyed it as much as your baby, put some time aside every day and introduce massage into your daily nursing routine from now on.

CHAPTER SEVEN

SENSUAL MASSAGE

Sensual massage is first and foremost gentle touching and stroking between partners. This type of contact is reassuring and caring. It helps to instigate tactile understanding between the two individuals. It also brings with it the comfort and confidence of being attractive enough to be touched. This is not only a comforting thought to the person being touched, but also to the one who is allowed and, indeed, encouraged to touch as a sign of a special intimate relationship between the two human beings. It can become a sensually electrifying experience.

This type of touch may mean loving, caressing and adoring. It is the action which words sometimes cannot express – there is no substitute for sensual touch. A very intimate, private and only one-to-one tactile experience is satisfying and relaxing. It helps to evoke a loving mood where two individuals develop deep self-esteem in an atmosphere of personal enhancement. Sensual massage has to be gentle and caring. It has to take place in the right atmosphere and it is up to you to create this atmosphere.

THE ART OF SENSUAL MASSAGE

Touch stimulates our senses in more ways than one. Imagine the amount of tension in your facial muscles after a tiring day in the office, where you had to keep smiling although you felt like crying. Imagine the amount of tension accumulated in your facial muscles when the bank manager refused you a loan and you could not stop smiling because the first one was not repaid yet. Think about how tense your facial muscles must be at the end of a long car journey full of traffic jams and motorway roadworks.

Relax and enjoy this practical part of sensual massage. In the following introduction to the art of sensual massage, a good way to start is by relaxing your facial muscles and perhaps, time permitting, your solar plexus which is situated in the abdominal cavity, behind the stomach. The solar plexus is the headquarters of our emotional life, and the abdominal area is a very sensitive part of the human body.

AROMATIC OILS

You may decide to use aromatic oils for this massage. Choose oils that will enhance the quality of your sensual massage. The fragrance has to appeal to the olfactory nerve of your partner. Make sure that the aroma is appreciated.

- For women, you could try Rose, Neroli,

Above: gentle and caring sensual massage between partners can enhance their relationship and help them both to relax together.

Lavender, Ylang Ylang, Jasmine, Grapefruit and most of the citrus oils.

■ For men, essential oils such as Sandalwood, Patchouli, Vetivert, Cedarwood and Rosewood would be more appropriate for their aphrodisiac qualities.

THE ENVIRONMENT

A warm room, subdued light, relaxing music and clean, warm towels are essential for creating a relaxing environment for you and your partner in order to create some quiet time together and enhance this session.

FACE MASSAGE

This sequence will help to relax the face, iron out the wrinkles and tone up the neck. The skin will look better and firmer with a healthy glow to it when the massage is finished. If you decide to include the top of the shoulders, the result will be total tranquillity, coupled with satisfaction and happiness.

1 With your partner in a supine position (facing the ceiling), start with a gentle touch on the top of the head, coming down the cheeks and finishing on the jawline. To do the massage, you can stand or sit down (if performed on the bed or the floor) at the top of your partner's head facing the toes.

1

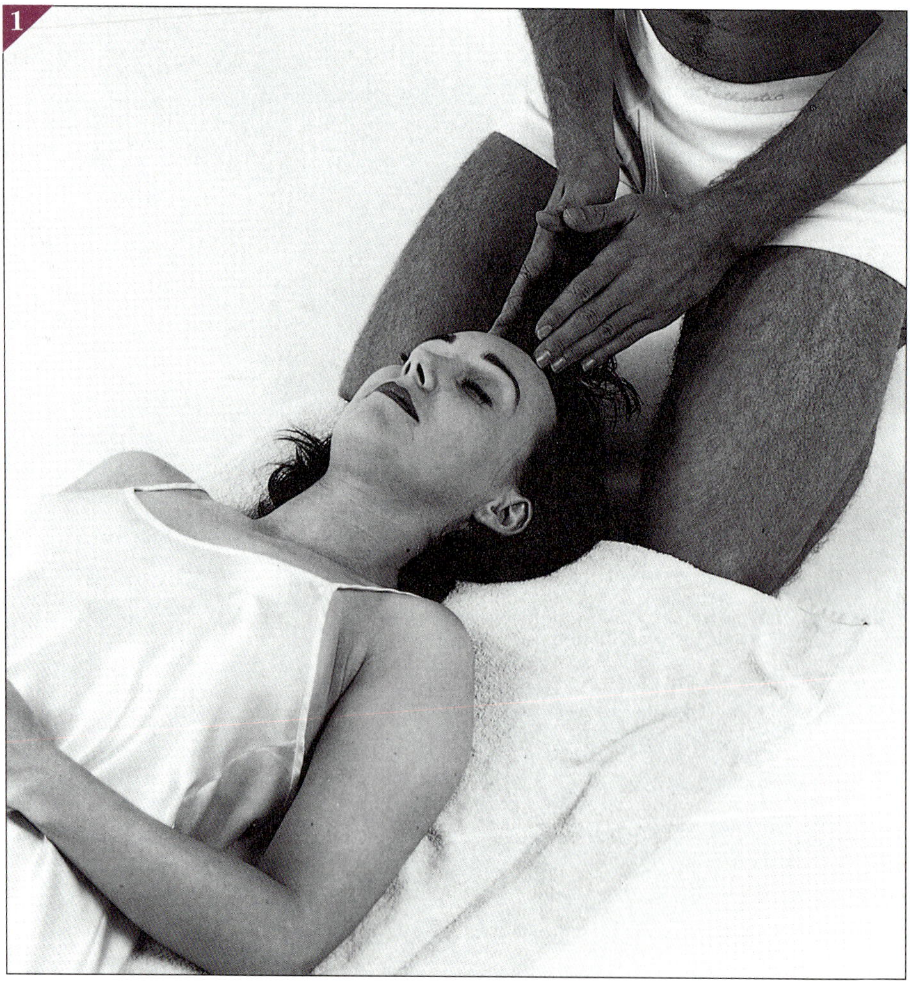

2 Apply a small amount of oil very lightly over the whole area of the face and neck. Start with gentle upward effleurage on the face and neck. Massage the eyelids with your ring fingers in very small circular motions with very gentle pressure. Stroke up the forehead with alternate hands (the fingers should lie across the forehead). Slide both hands towards the temples, applying gentle pressure there.

3 With fingers on the sides of the head (at ear level) place both thumbs, one on top of the other, between the eyebrows. Pressing down firmly, move higher up towards the hairline.

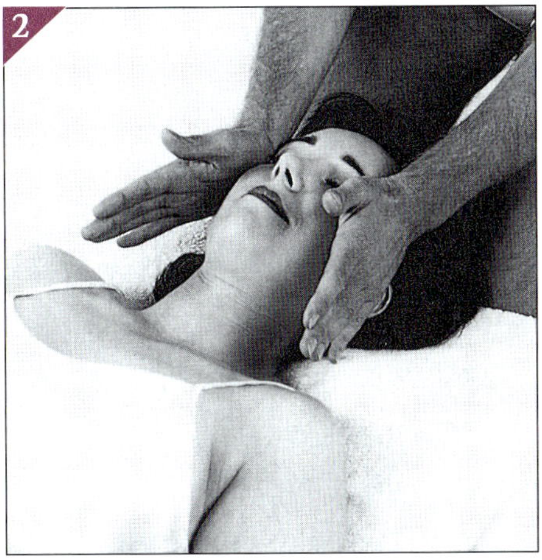

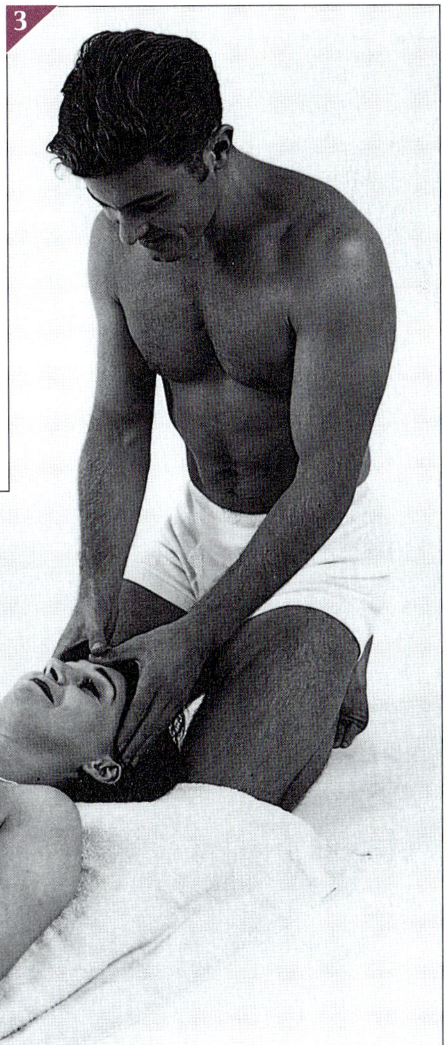

4 Place the thumbs at the base of the nose and stroke alternately with both thumbs from eyebrow level to the hairline.

5 With both thumbs on the sides of the eyebrows (thumbs side by side), move gradually towards the temples pressing gently and releasing – do not lose contact with the skin on the releasing action).

6 Place your hands on both sides of the head, with the fingers facing down and the thumbs parallel to each other in the middle of the forehead. Glide gently with the thenar muscles (the lower part of the thumb) to the side with your fingers in

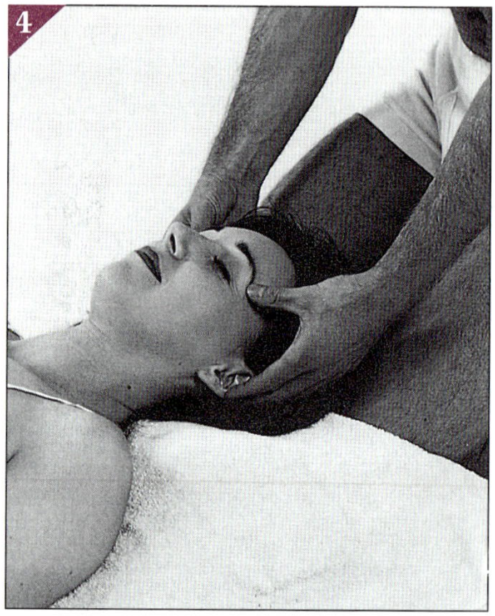

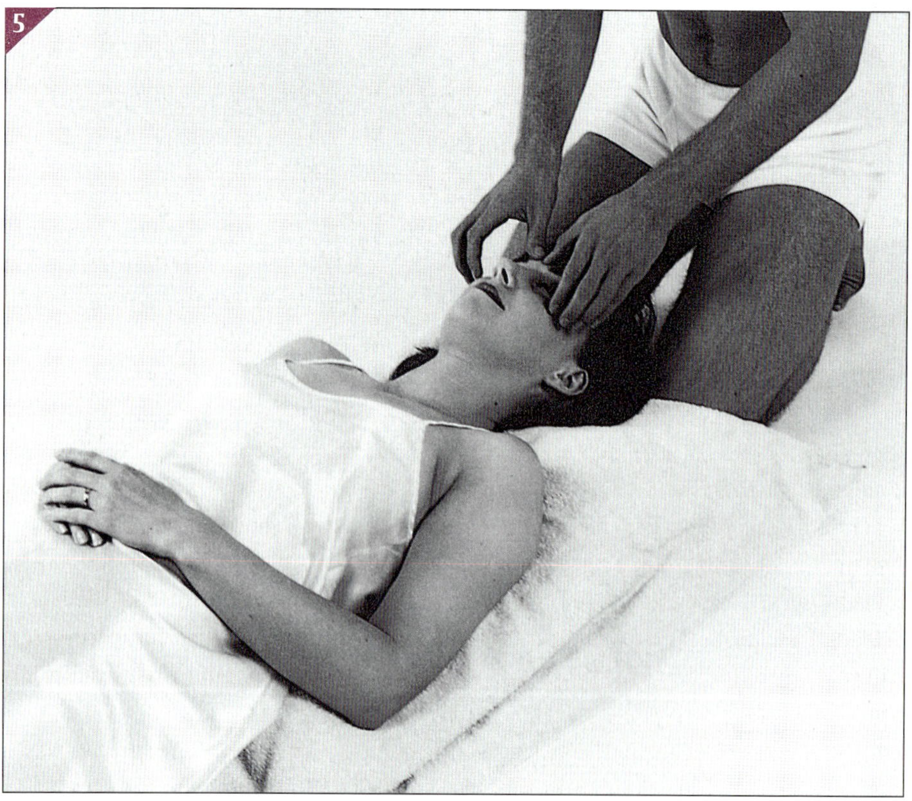

6
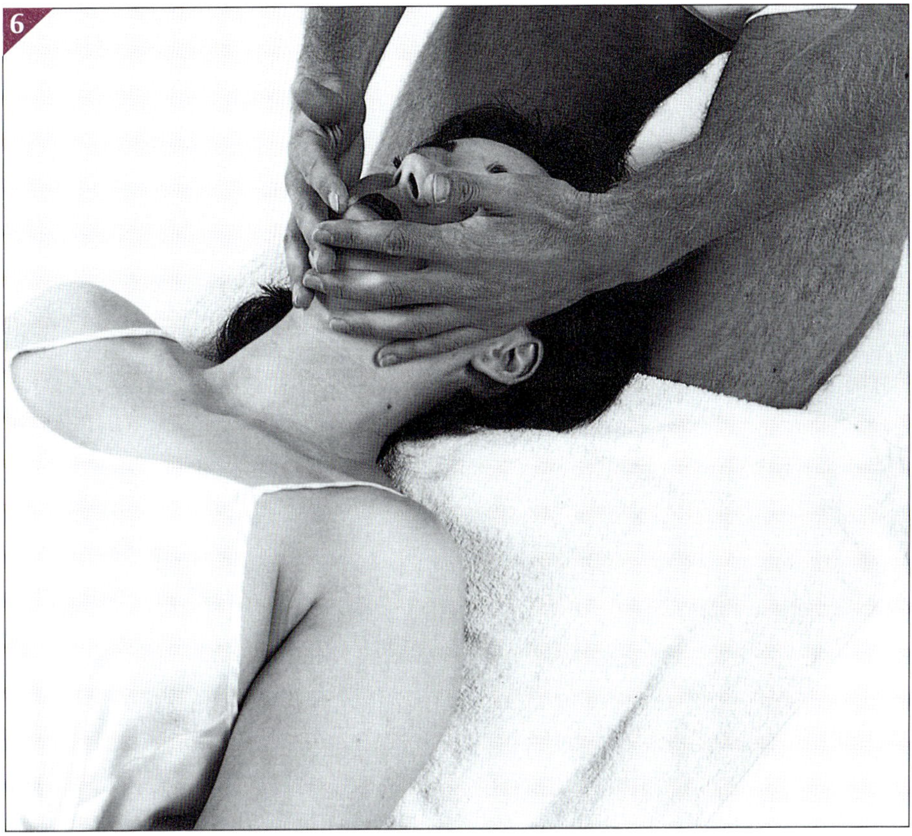

contact with the cheeks and jawline. Cup the head of your partner in both hands at the end of this stroke in stillness and hold for a moment. Attune to your partner's breathing and enjoy this moment of quiet togetherness.

Let the two thenar muscles meet in the centre of the forehead and slide gently out to the temples.

Place the thumbs on the forehead and, with your outstretched fingers of both hands on top of the cheekbone, effleurage gently to the sides several times. Mould your fingers to the shape of the cheekbone. When finished, rest the palms of your hands at temple level, hold the face between your hands, attune to the breathing pattern of your partner and relax. Peaceful stillness aids relaxation and intimacy.

Hold both cheeks with your cupped hands and, with the outstretched fingers of both hands, clasp them in an embrace at the middle of the jawline and slide gently to the sides of the bone, parting the fingers as you move your wrist in an outward movement.

Apply effleurage over the face area with both hands simultaneously by sliding the palms down the sides of the cheeks until the fingers of both hands meet at the middle of the jaw bone. Place the heels of the hands in the middle of the forehead again and, gliding downwards on both sides, let your fingers meet and clasp at midline of the jaw bone. Part the fingers of both hands and effleurage the neck area.

7 Place the top of the shoulder in between your thumbs and fingers with

the heels of the hands on both sides of the neck, and gently stroke downwards towards the shoulder joint and over.

8 Come back on the return stroke over the sternum and to the top of the neck, parting the hands to a fork position to start the downward movement again.

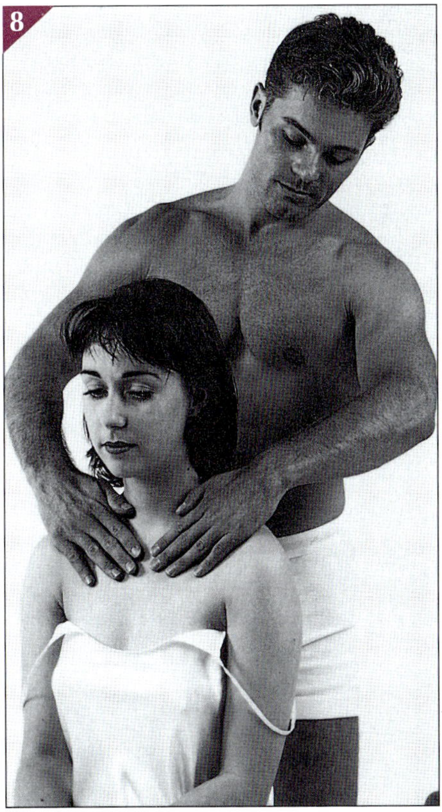

9 Effleurage with both hands at sternum level, stroking towards the shoulder joints with both hands. Place your fingers under the shoulder blade with thumbs on top of the shoulder area, and move the fingers up the neck on both sides.

Glide gently upwards to the top of the

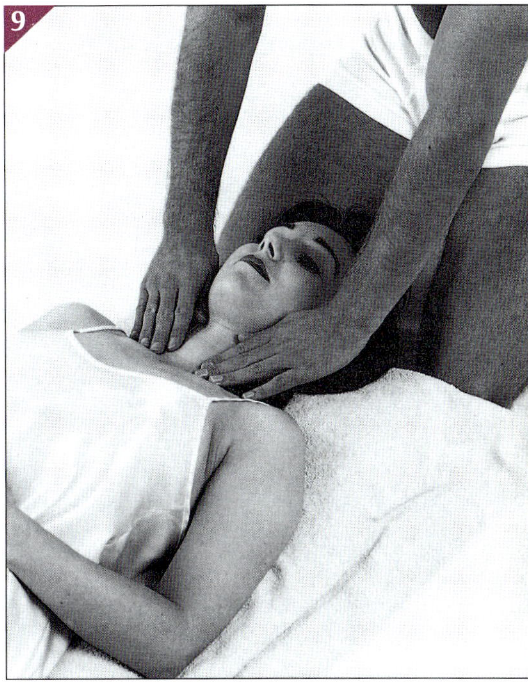

forehead and rest your hands in a relaxed comfortable position.

ACHIEVING DEEP RELAXATION

You should be able to hear your partner's heartbeat. You may find that your partner is relaxed so deeply that it would be unfair to terminate the contact. Wait with your hands in contact with the face and gently deposit a loving kiss on your partner's lips. The reaction you will receive will tell you everything about your skills as a body therapist. However, if your kiss is not reciprocated, do not despair. Practice, practice and more practice is necessary to achieve great heights of glory. So work hard towards the glory by learning the art of abdominal massage.

THE ABDOMEN

In the East the abdomen is referred to as the 'hara' and the massage of the hara is called ampulcu therapy. In ampulcu therapy, pressure is not applied with the thumbs and you should not remove your hands abruptly from the abdomen nor lose contact with the skin. The abdomen houses the solar plexus and it is a very sensitive area of the body. When finishing abdominal massage, place both hands on the navel area, stop, wait, and slowly lift the hands – do not withdraw them suddenly.

1 Apply medium pressure over the abdomen with some gentle effleurage movement up to the ribcage.

1

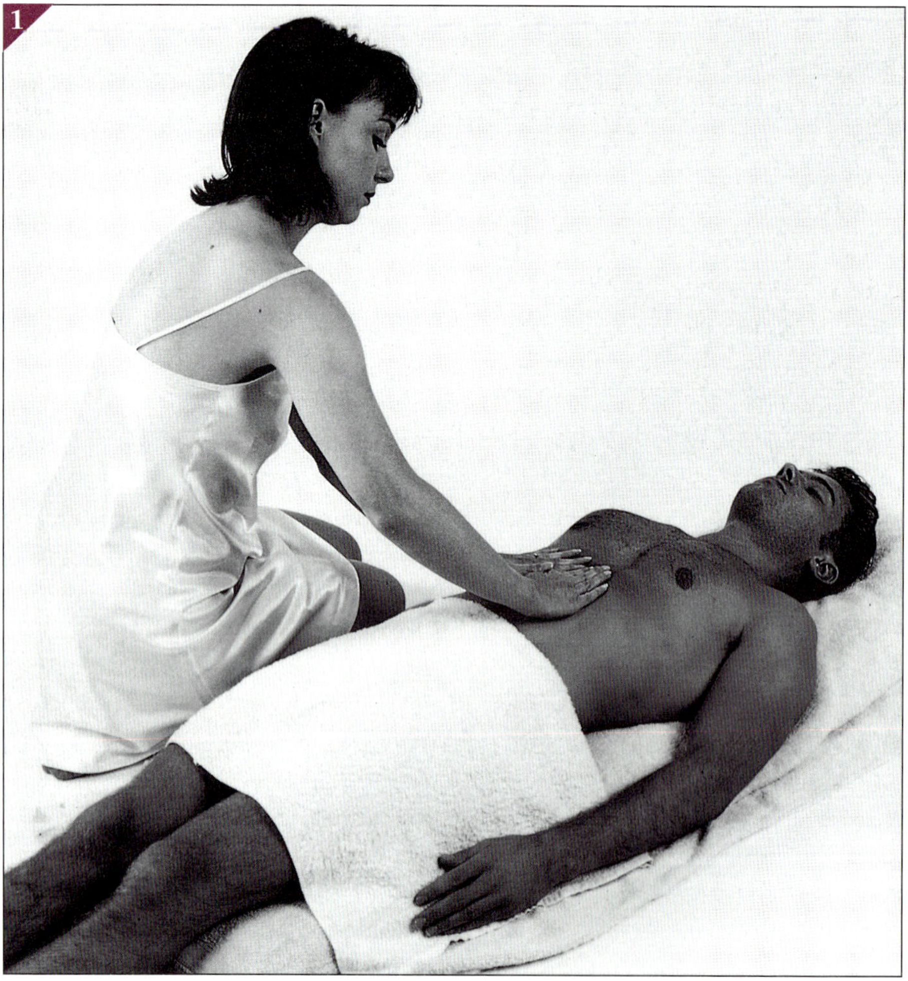

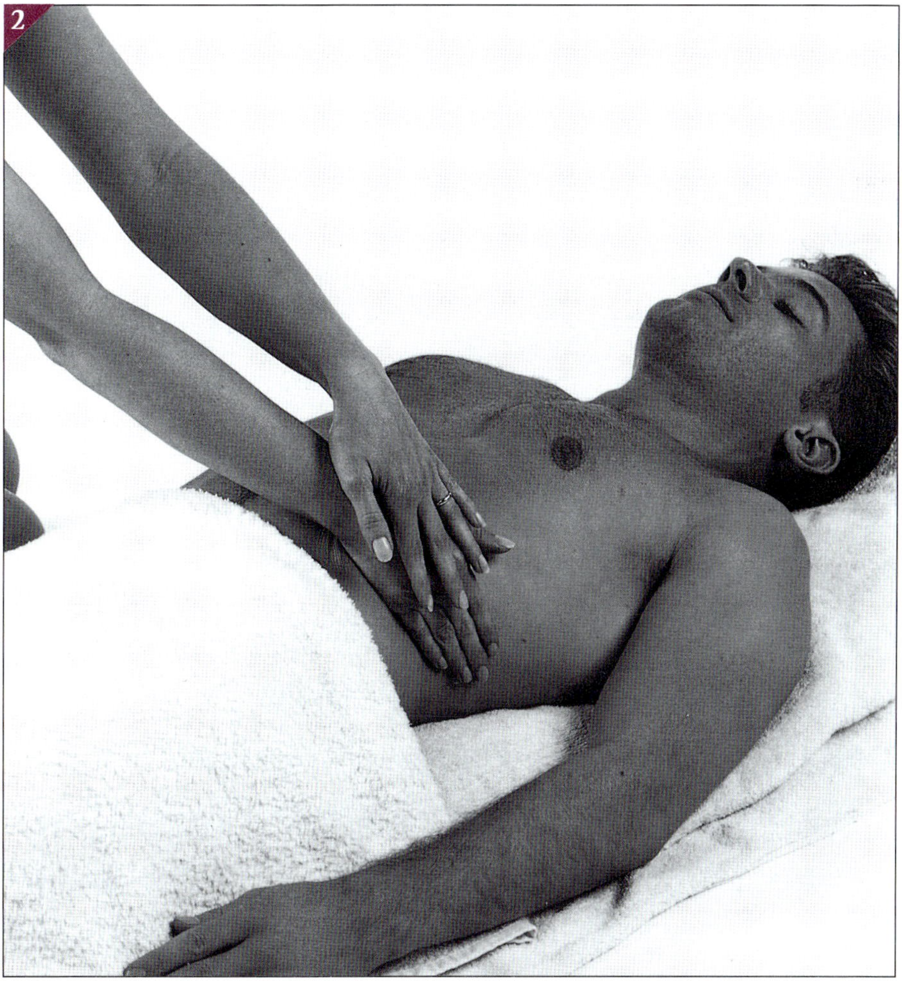

2 Place one hand on top of the other (fingers facing the head) and move gently outwards under the ribcage, turning the fingers to the side and under the waist.

3 Lift the body with slight pressure and, with the heels of the hands leading the movement, pull the hands down and inwards to the pelvic bone. This is a diamond-shaped movement and it can be repeated *ad lib*.

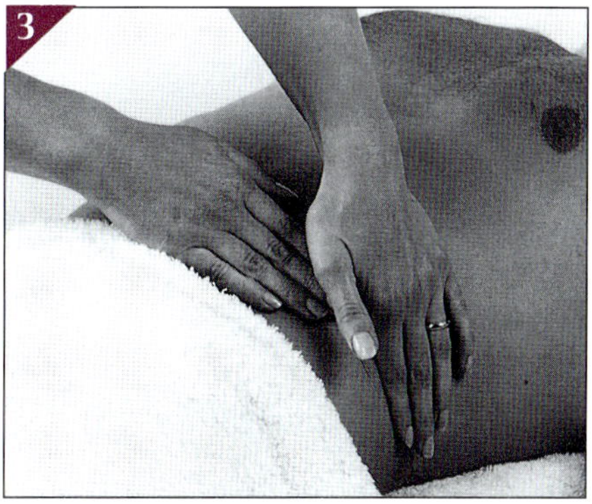

4 Using the outside edge of both hands, stroke down the abdomen below the left ribcage and then below the right side of the ribcage alternately.

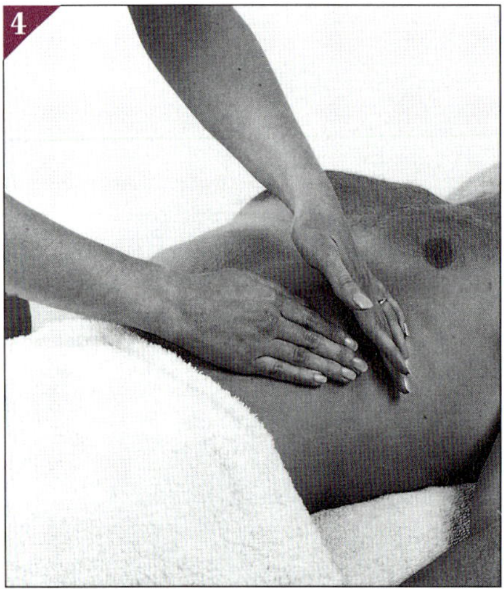

5 Place both hands on the right bottom corner of the abdomen and, in a clockwise oval movement with alternate hands, apply effleurage in a fluent, slow, rhythmical and gentle way over the whole area, so that your partner can relax fully.

6 Place both hands on one side of the ribcage with the heels resting on the ribs and fingers facing down. Perform effleurage up the sides of the ribcage with your fingers alternating – each time moving gradually one width of hand lower down the side of the waist and reaching the ilium level. Then perform the same movement on the other side of the body.

Return to the starting side and, with one hand on top of the other, apply small circular

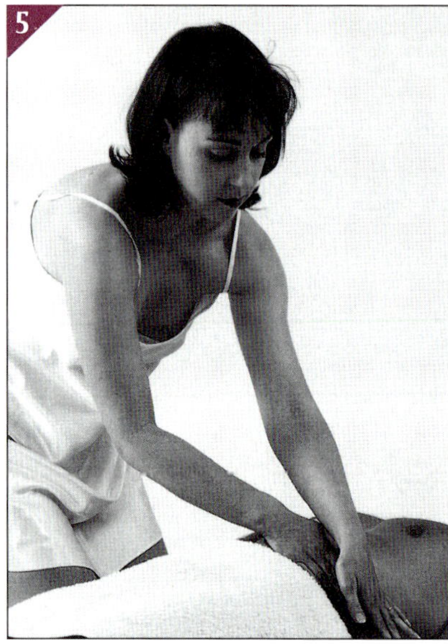

strokes moving down the side each time. Then move to the other side of the body and repeat the sequence.

Effleurage the abdomen and place the palm of the leading hand on top of the navel with your fingers in the direction of your body. Move the palm of the hand with the fingers in a clockwise direction from the wrist, with the heel of the hand stationary over the navel. Repeat several times and stop on the last stroke.

Place both hands on top of each other and relax. Keep in contact for some time and lift the hands off the body.

Cover the abdomen with a warm towel and await a response from your partner. Words of praise should be directed your way. Well done! And if you enjoyed it as much as your partner, now it is your partner's turn to reciprocate and give you a sensual massage.

6

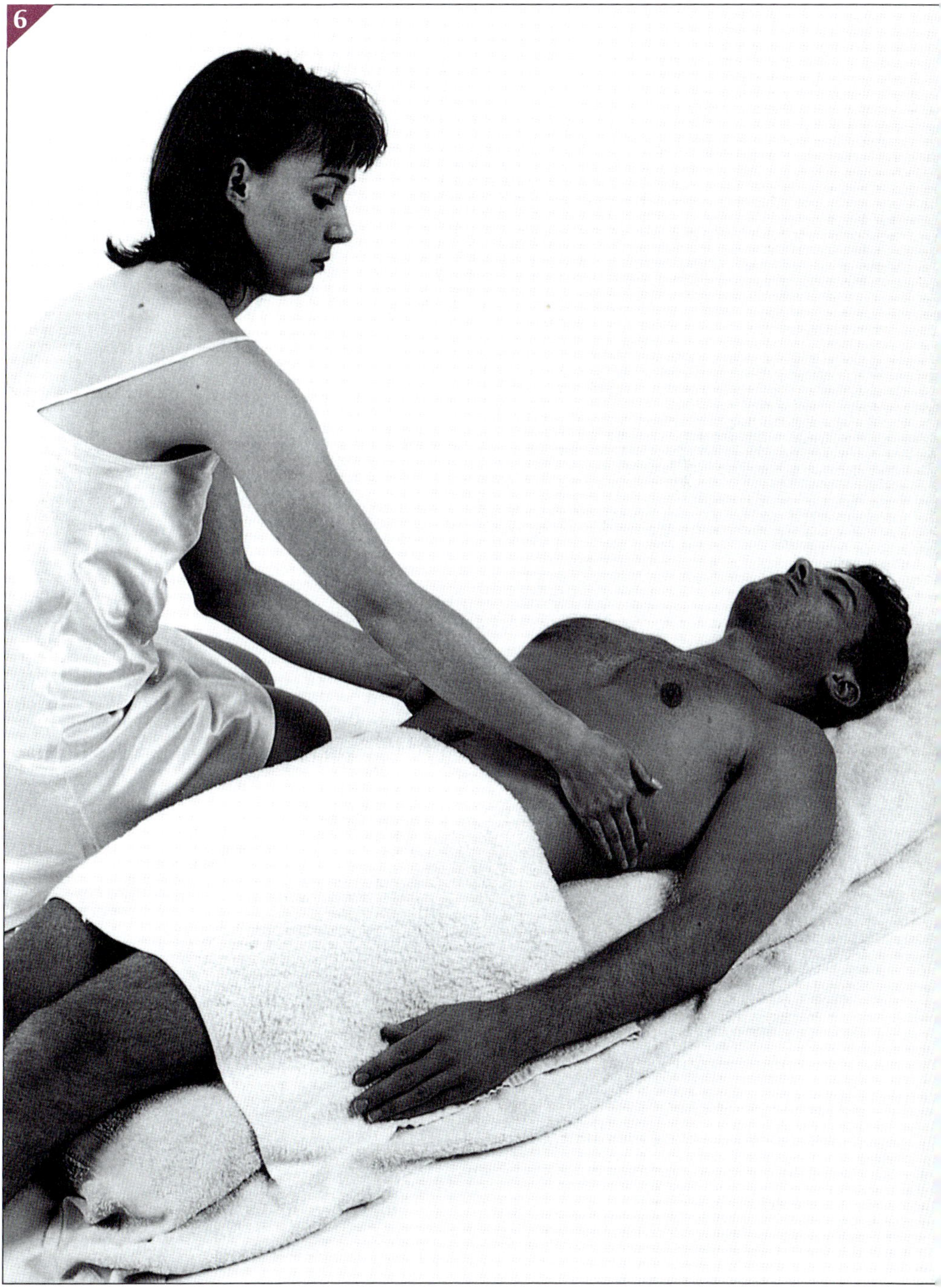

USEFUL ADDRESSES

UNITED KINGDOM

For information on courses in most forms of Complementary Medicine, contact:

The Institute for Complementary Medicine
Unit 15
Tavern Quay
Commercial Centre
Rope Street
London SE16 1TX
Tel: 0171 237 5165
Fax: 0171 237 5175

For information on registered practitioners in most forms of Complementary Medicine, you should contact:

The British Register of Complementary Practitioners
PO Box 194
London SE16 1QZ
Tel/fax: 0171 237 5175

BRCP Divisions include:
Aromatherapy, Chromotherapy, Colour, Chinese Medicine, Energy Medicine, Counselling, Healing Counselling, Herbal Medicine, Homeopathy, Medical Hypnotherapy, Psychotherapy, Indian Medicine, Japanese Medicine, Physical Medicine (Alexander Technique, Osteopathy, Chiropractic, Remedial Massage, Massage, Nutritional Medicine, Reflexology and others), Diagnostic systems: Iridology, Kinesiology, Signalysis. Professional techniques include: Heller Work, Rolfing, Bach Flower Remedies, Bates Eye Care.

AROMATHERAPY

International Federation of Aromatherapists
Stamford House
2–4 Chiswick High Road
London
W4 1TH

AUSTRALIA

Association of Massage Therapists
19a Spit Road
Mosman
NSW 2088

Association of Remedial Masseurs
22 Stuart Street
Ryde
NSW 2112

International Federation of Aromatherapists (Australian branch) Inc.
5 Uren Place
Kambahact 2902
Australia
Tel/fax: Australia 06 231 0707

UNITED STATES

AROMATHERAPY

National Association for Holistic Aromatherapy
219 Carl Street
San Francisco
CA 94117–3804
Tel: (415) 564–6785

MASSAGE

American Massage Therapy Association
820 Davis Street, Suite 100
Evanston
IL 60201–4444
Tel: (708) 864–0123

Associated Bodywork and Massage Professionals
28677 Buffalo Park Road
Evergreen
CO 80439–7347
Tel: (303) 674–8478

The Feldenkrais Guild
PO Box 489
Albany
OR 97321
Tel: (800) 775–8478

Body of Knowledge/Hellerwork
406 Berry Street
Mt. Shasta
CA 96067
Tel: (916) 926–2500
Fax: (916) 926–6839

International Association of Infant Massage
2350 Bowen Road
Elma
NY 14059
Tel: (800) 248–5432

NATUROPATHY

American Association of Naturopathic Physicians
2366 Eastlake Avenue
E Suite 322
Seattle
WA 98102
Tel: (206) 323–7610

OSTEOPATHY

American Osteopathic Association
142 E Ontario Street
Chicago
IL 60611

REFLEXOLOGY

International Institute of Reflexology
PO Box 12642
St. Petersburg
FL 33733–2642
Tel: (813) 343–4811

ROLFING

The Rolf Institute of Structural Integration
205 Canyon Boulevard
Boulder
CO 80302
Tel: (800) 530–8875

FURTHER READING

Arnould-Taylor, W.E., *A Textbook of Holistic Aromatherapy* (Stanley Thornes, 1992)

Arnould-Taylor, W.E., *The Principals and Practice of Physical Therapy* (Arnould Taylor Education Ltd., 1982)

Basnyet, J.C., *Healing by Feeling* (Jolanta Health Products, 1995)

Basnyet, J.C., *Manual of Carrier Oils* (Lancashire Holistic College, 1993)

Davis, P., *Subtle Aromatherapy* (C.W. Daniel Ltd., 1992)

Gillanders, A., *Reflexology, A Step-By-Step Guide* (Gaia Books Limited, 1995)

International School of Aromatherapy, *A Safety Guide on the Use of Essential Oils* (1993)

Jackson, A.J., *Alternative Health – Massage Therapy* (Optima, 1993)

Kurz, I., *Textbook of Dr. Vodder's Manual Lymph Drainage, Vol.III* (Haug)

Lautie, R., and Passebecq, A., *Aromatherapy: The Use of Plant Essences in Healing* (Thorsons, 1979)

Lawless, J., *The Encyclopaedia of Essential Oils* (Element, 1992)

McCarthy, M. (Ed), *Natural Therapies – The Complete A–Z of Complementary Medicine* (Thorsons, 1994)

Melzack, R., and Wall, D., *Pain Mechanism: a New Theory Science 150971* (Saffron Walden, 1965)

Valnet, J., *The Practice of Aromatherapy*

Vickers, A., *Massage and Aromatherapy – A Guide for Health Professionals* (Chapman & Hall, 1996)

INDEX